Never Throw Out a Banana Again

Never Throw Out a Banana Again

and 364 Other Ways to Save Money at Home Without Knocking Yourself Out

Darcie Sanders
and Martha M. Bullen

Crown Trade Paperbacks / New York

Some of the ideas in this book are unusual and creative. Many of them are purely original, while others were culled from family, friends, and other self-appointed savings experts. While to the best of our knowledge, none of it is illegal or unsafe, the information in this book is not intended to replace medical, financial, legal, or other professional advice. We expect our readers to exercise their normal good judgment when using the ideas in this book, and to take reasonable precautions as they deem necessary.

Published by Crown Trade Paperbacks, 201 East 50th Street, New York, New York 10022. Member of the Crown Publishing Group.

Random House, Inc. New York, Toronto, London, Sydney, Auckland

Manufactured in the United States of America

Design by Jennifer Harper

Library of Congress Cataloging-in-Publication Data
Sanders, Darcie
Never throw out a banana again : and 364 other ways to save money at home without knocking yourself out / by Darcie Sanders and Martha M. Bullen. — 1st ed.
p. cm.
1. Consumer education. 2. Home economics—Accounting.
I. Bullen, Martha M. II. Title. III. Title: 364 other ways to save money at home.
TX335.S195 1995
640'.42—dc20 94-20942
CIP

ISBN 0-517-88233-7

10 9 8 7 6 5 4 3 2 1

First Edition

CONTENTS

PREFACE

Money, money, money. For a long time, we were interested in making as much of it as we could. Then we acquired husbands, houses, and children. We finally realized that the most important factor in a solid financial foundation is not how much you *make* but how much you *keep*.

As we traveled the rocky road to financial frugality, we found plenty of advice but not much practical wisdom. Sure, we could save thousands if we dressed the kids in sacks or spent hours grinding our own flour, but we were looking for simple ways to cut down on our spending without knocking ourselves out.

Finally we put out the word to friends, family, colleagues, neighbors: Give us your favorite money-saving tips and strategies, the little things you do every day. And we got them! This book offers the refreshing and empowering message that taking small actions daily to cut your expenses can really pay off.

We've got the numbers to prove it. By using tips 19, 30, and 80, for example, you can easily save up to $1,000 a year. And that's just the beginning—you still have 362 more tips to try.

In Your Kitchen

Cooking Creatively on the Cheap

1. Never throw out a banana again.

There is literally no such thing as a "too-ripe banana." If it's just starting to get soft, slice it, place the pieces on waxed paper, and freeze them for a quick treat. For an extra-special snack, melt some chocolate or carob in a small saucepan and dip half of each banana slice before freezing. If the banana is really soft, peel it, smash it up a bit with a fork, scrape it into a plastic container, and freeze it until you're ready to bake delicious banana bread or muffins—or give it to your hungry baby or toddler.

2. Use it twice for half the price.

Leftovers, leftovers, leftovers. Everyone tells you to use leftovers, but the truth is that, in a casserole, they still look like leftovers. Our families got wise to mystery meat in layers real quick. Made into a tasty soup, however, leftovers are quite another thing.

Keep a large plastic tub in your freezer and add leftovers (such as turkey wings, macaroni, carrots, and potatoes) all week long. Come Friday night, toss the frozen mixture into a pot of water with some spices and maybe even some beans, simmer for several hours, and voilà! a hearty and inexpensive Saturday lunch or Sunday supper magically appears. When a tantalizing smell comes wafting from the pot, your family will think you've spent hours slaving over the stove.

Terry-cloth "vegetable crisper bags," which are supposed to keep vegetables crisp and dry, sell for $6 apiece. You would need to buy several bags to store all the fresh vegetables and fruit a family goes through each week—or you can try our cheap sponge trick, which costs about 39 cents.

3. Keep fruit fresh longer.

What's the use of getting a great deal on a bushel of peaches, only to have half of them develop an interesting glow-in-the-dark purple fuzz because they spoiled before you could eat them?

An easy and inexpensive way to keep vegetables and fruits fresh longer is to put a dry sponge in the refrigerator bin with them to absorb the excess moisture that encourages spoilage.

4. Meal planning 101.

Get in the habit of doing a weekly fridge inventory before you shop (perhaps while you're making your grocery shopping list). You'll be surprised how often you'll find fresh fruit, cheese, half-eaten jars of applesauce, or other perishables that you'd forgotten about lurking in the back. Then you can plan a meal around these foods and use them up *before* they turn green or mushy and you have to throw them out.

Here's a few ways to incorporate food you already have in your favorite family meals:

- Add extra veggies (such as broccoli, carrots, peas, or celery) to pasta, or make vegetarian chili.
- Blend bananas, berries, or other fruits with milk and a little vanilla ice cream or frozen yogurt to make a delicious (and reasonably healthful) milk shake.
- Turn stale bread into French toast—or crumble old bread to make bread crumbs to use in casseroles and for fried chicken.

- Create a comforting pudding from leftover rice—just add a tablespoon of honey, a little milk, one beaten egg, and a handful of raisins, mix with a pinch of cinnamon and nutmeg, and heat in the microwave or on the stovetop for 5 minutes.

5. Foiled again.

Line the floor of your oven when you're making home-cooked pizza, fruit pies, or casseroles, which might burble over and make a mess of your oven. (Remember not to cover the *entire* floor, since that would interfere with even heat distribution.) Using the foil as an oven liner means you'll rarely have to buy oven cleaners (which cost around $3.50 for 16 ounces). You'll also save yourself a lot of elbow grease to keep your oven free from baked-on grunge.

6. Lean on beans.

Use one of the cheapest and most nutritious foods—dried beans—in your cooking. Many people are reluctant to buy dried beans, though, because soaking them overnight is such a bother.

Here's a quick way to get beans going that will let you use them in a same-night recipe: Instead of soaking the beans, scald them in boiling water. This greatly reduces the subsequent cooking time (and reportedly helps with gasiness, too). The trick to scalding beans is to add them to the boiling water s-l-o-w-l-y, so that the boiling never stops. Boil hard for 15 minutes, then season. Now they're ready to use in your favorite recipes. We like to use these beans in Chili con Carne. (Simmer the beans with ground beef, a can of tomatoes, chili powder, chopped green pepper and onion, and serve on rice.) We also add beans, chili peppers, and Monterey Jack cheese to pasta to make a Tex-Mex special.

Dried beans at 50 cents a pound cost half of what canned refried beans cost ($1.05 a pound)—and your refried beans won't be made with artery-clogging lard, as many of the canned ones are.

GREEN FETTUCCINE WITH GREEN ONIONS

4 tablespoons butter or margine

1 cup diced green onions

2 cloves garlic, minced

Carrots (optional)

Cherry tomatoes (optional)

Green or red peppers (optional)

3–4 cups green fettuccine, cooked

1 cup whipping cream or half-and-half

1 cup freshly grated Parmesan or Romano cheese

Salt

Pepper

Nutmeg

Melt the butter or margarine in a skillet or wok.

Add the diced green onions and minced garlic, plus carrots, tomatoes, and green or red peppers, if desired, and stir-fry for about 2 minutes.

Add the cooked fettuccine and the cream or half-and-half. Cook, stirring frequently, over high heat for 2 to 3 minutes. Add the grated cheese. Season to taste with salt, pepper, and nutmeg, and serve with additional grated cheese on top. This dish is best accompanied by hot garlic bread and a salad.

Serves 4

7. Think vegetarian!

No, you don't have to trade in your burgers for beansprouts all the time, but meat is usually the most expensive source of protein. If you plan just one (or two) vegetarian meals a week, you can cut down on your grocery store bills significantly. Most children love pasta and rice, two veggie staples, and they're quicker

BLUE CHEESE CAULIFLOWER

1 head cauliflower

3 stalks celery

2 tablespoons margarine

2 tablespoons flour

1 cup milk

2 green onions, diced

4 tablespoons blue cheese, crumbled

1 cup plain bread crumbs

Pepper to taste

2 tablespoons grated Parmesan cheese

Cut the cauliflower into flowerets and dice the celery.

Add water to cover, then boil both in the same saucepan over medium heat until tender (about 10–15 minutes).

Place the vegetables in an over-proof serving dish.

In a small saucepan, melt the margarine over low heat. Stir in the flour and cook for 1 minute.

Whisk in the milk and cook over medium-high heat until the sauce thickens.

Stir in the diced green onions.

Remove from the heat and pour over the vegetables.

In a small bowl, mix together the blue cheese, bread crumbs, and pepper and Parmesan cheese. Sprinkle over the vegetables in the serving dish.

Broil the cauliflower mixture until the topping is golden brown.

Serves 4 as a main dish

and easier to prepare than most meat dishes—which is certainly a bonus for the cook in the family.

REFRIED BEAN AND PEPPER BURRITOS

1 tablespoon vegetable or olive oil

1 small onion, chopped

1 clove garlic, minced

1 large green pepper, chopped

1 12-ounce can cooked kidney beans *or* 1 12-ounce can refried beans

2 teaspoons chili powder

½ teaspoon ground cumin

1 teaspoon oregano

Seasoned salt

Pepper

8 large flour tortillas

1 cup Monterey Jack or cheddar cheese, grated

Mild chili sauce to taste

Lettuce

2 medium tomatoes, chopped

Sour cream or guacamole

Heat the vegetable or olive oil in a skillet over medium heat. Add the onion and garlic. Cook for abut 5 minutes.

Add the green pepper and cook 5 minutes more.

Drain and mash the kidney beans, then add them to the skillet. (Or add the refried beans straight from the can.) Season the mixtue with chili powder, cumin, and oregano, plus seasoned salt and pepper to taste.

Heat the mixture for about 5 minutes.

Fill the flour tortillas with the mixture, then top each tortilla with a spoonful of grated cheese. Roll up each tortilla and place them all in a large rectangular

(continued)

microwave-proof baking dish. Top the tortillas with chili sauce and extra grated cheese.

Heat the tortillas in the microwave on medium heat for 5 minutes.

Serve the burritos with shredded lettuce and chopped tomatoes and a dollop of sour cream or guacamole.

Serves 4

8. Who needs this?

Recently we saw foil-lined bags advertised in a catalog as "Fat Trappers" for leftover cooking grease. Five bags plus a nifty little plastic container were being sold for $9.95. Ten extra bags could be purchased at $4.95. Sounded great, until we realized that those bags are available for free when you buy whole-bean coffee. Now we have a great way to recycle the bags when the coffee's gone. Of course, our moms still use the traditional Fat Trappers—empty frozen juice cans, instant coffee jars, or ground coffee cans. Whatever container you use, draining the grease whenever you cook meat will save the kitchen sink, the pipes, and your arteries from getting all clogged up.

9. Who needs this?

For about $13, you can buy two plastic "microwave dome lids" to cover your dishes in the microwave—or you can buy a roll of plastic wrap for $1.99, which serves the same purpose. Better yet (for your pocketbook and the environment), invert one bowl over another and create your own "dome" for free. This trick works especially well for steaming vegetables and reheating soups, casseroles, or cold pasta. Another cheap, reusable microwave method is to turn a paper plate upside down over the dish to help the food cook faster.

10. Here's another microwave "Who needs this?"

A "no-mess bacon cooker." It includes Teflon hanging racks and a fancy splatter shield—all this for only $39.95. Or, for a couple of cents, you could put 1 paper towel on one of your regular kitchen plates, place a few bacon strips on it, cover the bacon with two more paper towels and get exactly the same results. (Microwave at 1 minute per bacon slice for extra-crispy bacon; cook for 30 to 45 seconds per slice if you don't like it quite so crunchy.)

11. Chill out with homemade ice pops.

Instead of buying chemically colored, nutritionally bankrupt grocery store ice pops, why not make your own? For a couple of dollars, you can buy a plastic ice pop freezer tray, and pour in your own economical juice from frozen concentrate. (Orange, grape, cherry, and lemonade are healthy kid-pleasers.) Your ice pop maker will last you summer after summer. Or make your own ice pops with pudding, sherbet, yogurt, or blended fresh fruit and ice cream sticks. (Sticks are essential for little kids who can't handle a loose cube safely.) An added advantage is that juice cubes can be stockpiled in a plastic bowl in the freezer, where they're handy for a party or picnic.

If your children turn up their noses at drinking orange juice (the real thing, not the powdered variety), try this: When Martha's fifteen-year-old fridge went on the blink and started freezing all its contents, she was surprised to find that her daughter loved the slushy "orange shake." In fact, even after the refrigerator was fixed, her daughter still insists on having her glass of juice individually frozen!

12. Who needs this?

Our local hardware store is selling a Kitchen Fire Extinguisher for $15. All it contains is sodium bicarbonate—baking soda. Thank you very much, we'll take a pass on the avocado green wall-mount canister for $15 and just stick with our 69-cent box of Arm & Hammer (strategically positioned in the cabinet nearest the stove).

13. Munch on muffins.

Make up double batches of home-cooked muffins once every week or two to enjoy for breakfast. Not only are they much less expensive than store-bought processed cereals, they are tastier and can do double duty as snacks or treats to spice up your brown-bag lunch. Making one dozen muffins from scratch costs only $1.50. If you eat two muffins at a time, you'll have enough for six days' worth of breakfasts or lunches, at a cost of 25 cents per meal! You can store these muffins in the refrigerator for up to two weeks—or you can freeze them to enjoy later.

14. Don't send out for that pizza.

Too tired to cook? Don't automatically reach for the phone. By the time everyone chooses a topping, your "cheap-and-easy" pizza could easily cost you $15 or more.

For under $5 for a family of four, you can have a do-it-yourself pizza party instead. Use English muffins, bagels, tortillas, or refrigerated pizza dough as the base, homemade or store-bought spaghetti sauce, and several kinds of vegetables and cheese as the topping. Making your own lets you customize your pizzas to each family member's taste and also provides an opportunity to use up bits of leftovers hanging out in the fridge. Besides, mozzarella, feta, Jack, or brick cheeses are great on a pizza, as are leftover stir-fry vegetables.

LOW-CHOLESTEROL FRUITY BRAN MUFFINS

2¼ cups uncooked oat bran cereal

½ cup diced mixed dried fruit

1 teaspoon ground cinnamon

½ teaspoon ground nutmeg

1 teaspoon baking powder

½ teaspoon baking soda

¼ teaspoon salt

Whites from 2 large eggs (or use 1 whole egg)

1 cup applesauce

½ cup packed light brown sugar

½ cup buttermilk *or* plain, vanilla, or flavored yogurt

2 tablespoons vegetable oil

Preheat the oven to 350°.

Lightly spray 12 regular-size muffin cups with nonstick cooking spray or grease them with margarine.

Mix the oat bran, dried fruit, spices, baking powder and soda, and salt in a bowl.

In a large bowl, combine the remaining ingredients with a wooden spoon, stirring until well blended.

Add the oat bran mixture to the wet mixture, stirring to mix well. Spoon ⅓ cup batter into each muffin cup. (The muffin cups should be two-thirds full.)

Bake the muffins for 30–35 minutes, until they are lightly browned and spring back when pressed gently.

Cool on a wire rack.

Variations: Instead of mixed dried fruit, use raisins, bananas, blueberries, peaches, apples, or raspberries.

Makes 12 regular-size muffins or 24 minimuffins

An electric pizza oven is advertised as making homemade pizzas with crisp crusts in just 5 minutes. This sounds good until you look at the price tag: $225! We favor baking pizza on a beat-up cookie sheet in the oven like everyone else. Our secret for those crispy crusts: Preheat your sheet along with the oven.

15. Never, ever, ever put coffee grounds down your sink.

It's a sure-fire clog and an expensive mistake often requiring a plumber, especially if the grounds get into contact with any latent grease in your traps.

Okay, so you didn't follow the previous rule and poured coffee grounds down the sink right after cleaning up the Sunday morning bacon-and-eggs plates. Hoo boy, are you in trouble. But before you call the plumber or drag out your plumbing "snake," try this: Mix together ½ cup salt and ½ cup baking soda (not baking powder) and pour it down the drain. Then slowly pour at least 1 quart of boiling water down the drain. Sometimes you luck out (especially if the clog is composed mainly of small greasy bits and not an actual lump of something solid), and this will do the trick. If it works, you've just saved yourself between $55 and $75, which is what a plumber charges to accomplish the same thing. And what are you doing eating bacon and eggs and coffee, anyhow? Haven't you heard of heart attacks?

16. Use it twice for half the price.

When eating out, don't be ashamed to ask for a leftover bag. Last night's dinner makes a great lunch today—and it's food you've already paid for, which makes it doubly satisfying. The remains of a family's Chinese dinner can last for a couple of lunches if you cook up some more rice. And many of us adore cold pizza or spaghetti for breakfast! If the leftovers look less appealing the next day than you thought they would, well, that's one less bowl of dog or cat food you have to buy. Why do you think they call them doggie bags?

17. Give up soda.

Get into water or, if you're totally unable to give up the soda habit, switch to your grocery store's house brand instead of the more expensive nationally advertised name brands. Another alternative is to buy some of the more creatively flavored frozen fruit juices from your grocery store—including pineapple banana, cran-raspberry, wild cherry, and so on. You can give these drinks to your kids without feeling guilty about getting them hooked on soda.

We used to be serious soda addicts, going through a case a week at home and paying an extra dollar or so each when we ate out for the privilege of having our teeth coated in liquid sugar. Then one night we added it up: At $8 a week for the grocery purchase, with an additional $4 for the restaurant, we were spending $624 a year on flavored water—more than we spent on car tuneups or the kids' clothing.

Like many addicts, we had to ease off slowly—first with iced tea, then down to lemonade. At about $5 a week, tea and lemonade were cheaper, but not necessarily better for our teeth. As the weeks wore on, we mixed that lemonade thinner and thinner, until $5 of dry mix was lasting us a month. Finally, over a year later, we're pure water drinkers and proud of it.

18. Use inexpensive kitchen beauty potions.

The eggs and oil in mayonnaise will treat your hair as well as—or better than—store-bought conditioners. And at $1.59 a quart versus $2.99 for a single treatment, you can't beat the price.

Here's how to do it: Apply ¼ cup of mayo to dry, unwashed hair. (Use a little more for really long hair.) Comb through and then cover with a plastic shower cap. Sit under a hair dryer set on the lowest setting for about 10 minutes. Then turn off the dryer but keep the cap on for an additional 15 minutes. Rinse your hair thoroughly and then shampoo as usual. Your hair will be as fabulous as if you used the most expensive hot-oil treatment.

19. Eat cheap on the run.

Even if you are so rushed in the morning that you don't have the time to sit down, fine—there are plenty of economical and healthful breakfasts you can pocket to munch on the train, bus, car, or even on foot.

Example: A whole-wheat bagel smeared with cream cheese costs about 39 cents and is easily eaten one-handed while driving or running to the train station. Purchased at the train station breakfast bar, it costs $1.75 (plus you have to wait to get your change as the cashier breaks open another change roll). That's $1.35 in savings per day, which adds up to $6.85 a week, or over $300 per year just from breakfast for one person. You also can bring your own coffee from home in a Styrofoam cup with commuter top, or use a small thermos.

20. Make your own mac 'n' cheese.

Boiling your own macaroni and making a quick cheese sauce takes only 5 minutes longer than the packaged variety, tastes much better, costs only pennies per serving—and isn't such a lurid shade of orange. If you want to dress it up a bit for more adult tastes, add a few varieties of cheese (cheddar, Jack, and Parmesan work well), a little Dijon mustard, and green onions or fresh chives. For extra savings, use up any little dried-out ends of cheese on this dish—while they may be too tough for sandwiches, they melt down beautifully.

21. Bake in batches.

This saves on fuel and time. For example, you can put in a batch or two of muffins or banana bread after your dinner comes out of the oven; then you can enjoy them for dessert or during the coming week. When cooking dinner, you can use the preheated oven to make a meat loaf for tonight and a casserole for the next day. If you're *really* organized, you can cook several entrées over the weekend and then store them in your freezer for weekday meals. Microwave owners can zap these dishes quickly during the week and won't have to power up the oven at all.

TURKEY MARSALA

1 tablespoon olive oil

1 pound mushrooms, sliced

½ cup leftover gravy

1 cup coarsely chopped leftover turkey meat

¼ Marsala wine (or sherry)

Chicken broth or water

Rice, noodles, or toast, as desired

In a skillet, heat the oil over medium-high heat.

Add the mushrooms and sauté lightly.

Add the gravy, turkey, and wine. Simmer gently for 15 minutes, stirring frequently and adding chicken broth or water to taste if the sauce thickens too much.

Serve over rice, noodles, or toast.

Serves 4

22. Talk turkey.

It's too good—and cheap—to be eaten only on Thanksgiving. Besides great soup stock fixin's and less fat than beef, you also get more meat per pound than chicken, because turkeys have proportionally larger breasts and drumsticks. Nothing cheers a household up like the aroma of a turkey roasting in the oven. Just to remind you, here are three not-so-typical turkey recipes to use throughout the year:

TURKEY STIR-FRY

2 cups leftover turkey
Cornstarch
Carrots
Onions
Green or red peppers
Sweet potatoes
3 tablespoons vegetable oil
Chopped garlic
⅔ cup water or chicken broth
Soy sauce to taste
Sherry to taste
Rice or tortillas

Cut the turkey into strips about as wide as a pencil but half as long. Dredge the meat strips in the cornstarch.

Also cut the carrots, onions, peppers, and potatoes into strips.

Heat the oil in a skillet until hot, adding garlic to taste if desired.

Stir-fry the vegetables until tender-crisp, about 5 minutes.

Add the turkey and the water or chicken broth. Continue stirring, and add the soy sauce and sherry to taste.

Serve over rice or tortillas.

Serves 4

TURKEY HASH

1½ pounds red potatoes, chopped

1 tablespoon vegetable oil

1 large onion, chopped

2 medium green or red peppers, chopped

3 stalks celery, chopped

2 cups chopped leftover turkey

½ cup milk

Salt

Pepper

Poultry seasoning

Worcestershire sauce

4 fried eggs, if desired

Parboil the potatoes for 10 minutes. Drain.

Heat the vegetable oil in a large skillet.

Add the potatoes, onion, peppers, and celery. Sauté until the onions are clear, about 10 minutes.

Add the leftover turkey and milk, and season to taste with salt, pepper, poultry seasoning, and Worcestershire sauce. Continue cooking over low heat for another 10 minutes to blend the flavors.

Serve alone or with the traditional fried egg.

Serves 4

23. Here's berry good advice.

If you like to buy a lot of fresh berries in season at your local farmer's market, you can save some to enjoy later. Simply place dry, fresh berries on a baking sheet in a single layer, then put the baking sheet in your freezer. Once the berries are frozen, you can keep them in plastic bags and enjoy them for munching or baking throughout the year. And think what additional pleasure you'll have in the dead of winter knowing you're eating June blueberries at 49 cents a pint, instead of January ones at $3.98.

24. Bake your own cookies!

While this doesn't sound particularly frugal or self-denying, it sure beats paying for the brand name, little plastic trays, and all the other packaging that comes with store-bought cookies. For example, Keebler Chocolate Chip cookies are $3.05 a pound, while Pillsbury frozen dough costs only $2.12 a pound. Homemade dough costs well under $1 a pound. Of course, if you bake your own, you may not end up with as many cookies, because you have all those bonus bites of irresistible raw cookie dough.

25. Keep breakfast basic.

We all know that sugary cereals are lousy for you—but what is not often mentioned is how ridiculously expensive they are. Many cereals are topping the $4 mark lately. Instead of giving in to your kids' pleas for the latest multicolored breakfast cereal, buy your basic corn or wheat flakes (most stores have their own brand), which cost just 17¢ an ounce. Then add your own dried fruit, fresh fruit, and honey or sugar at home for a much more economical and healthier alternative.

For example, plain Rice Crispies cost $2.43 at our corner grocery. The Apples and Cinnamon version will set you back a whopping $3.99, while the generic brand costs only $1.99. A box of the generic cereal plus a $1 box of raisins and a dash of cinnamon from your spice cabinet will provide you with more fruit per serving at a 25 percent saving. Let's put it this way: Would you like to get every fourth box of cereal free?

26. Get the most nutrition for your money.

Buy your milk in cardboard instead of plastic containers. Why? Because the vitamin A and riboflavin in milk tend to break down under light, which cardboard containers block more effectively than clear plastic jugs. (If cardboard isn't available in your area, look for yellow plastic jugs. If neither is available, complain to your store manager.)

> **B**onus benefit: Old waxed paper milk cartons give you an opportunity for some serious recycling. Among the many uses for these cartons are: seed starter window boxes, pen and pencil organizers, workshop organizers, doll houses and model horse barns, and library shelves for minibooks. You can cover them with old wrapping paper or paint them for a cheerier look if you like.

27. Let's talk tofu.

You know the stuff, that bland block of soy milk cheese you probably can find in the gourmet or Oriental section of your grocery. Diehard vegetarians eat it straight, though we confess to finding it pretty tasteless. But that is tofu's great charm: It's bland but soaks up other flavors beautifully. Try cooking with a 50/50 blend of tofu and ground beef when making spaghetti, lasagna, chili, or other casseroles with tasty sauces. The flavor will be great, the cholesterol will be cut in half, your meat budget will be stretched—and your meals will be lower in fat. Ground beef costs around $2.89 a pound versus 99 cents a pound for tofu. If you use tofu just twice a week, you'll save $200 a year and never miss the meat.

28. Smart chefs stir-fry.

Food can cost you money even *after* you've purchased it. How? It's the money you spend on the cooking itself. What is the most energy-efficient—and therefore least costly—method of cooking? Stir-fried Oriental-type dishes in which the food is chopped fine and cooked quickly over a high flame make the best use of your energy dollars. In terms of equipment, microwave ovens and Crock-Pots really do earn their keep due to the efficiency of their cooking. The most expensive cooking appliances to operate are electric and toaster ovens, while gas ovens and electric frying pans fall somewhere in the middle.

If you want to reap the full benefit of your microwave's efficiency, keep it clean. All those spills, crumbs, and latticework of cheese bubbles absorb the energy waves just like the "real" food you are trying to cook, thereby increasing your cooking time and costs.

29. Skip the seasoning mix.

Don't waste 79 cents on taco seasoning mix every time you make a Mexican meal. Also, forget those handy tostada and enchilada seasoning packets. If you look closely at the back ingredient lists, you'll find that they all have exactly the same components! All of these seasoning mixes are nothing but common spices you'll find in your own cupboard. You can make your own for under 10 cents by combining 1 teaspoon each chili powder, cumin, cilantro, oregano, garlic powder, dried onions, and seasoning salt. If you cook Mexican just twice a week, your yearly savings will be about $75—more if you grow your own cilantro and oregano. Add a few sprinkles of black or red pepper and paprika (plus dried chili peppers if you like it really zippy), and you've

Okay, your mix will be missing the MSG, hydrolyzed vegetable protein, disodium inosinate, disodium guanylate, and tricalcium phosphate found in the dried mixes—but we think that's just as well.

created a tastier spice mix at a fraction of the cost. Store it in a plastic container or airtight plastic bag to keep it fresh for your next South-of-the-Border meal.

30. Save a bunch at lunch.

According to a survey by the National Restaurant Association, about 40 percent of American adults eat out or buy carry-out once or twice a week, and 12 percent indulge three or four times a week. If you must go out for a restaurant meal now and then, try to go at lunchtime. Many restaurants offer the same entrées as their dinnertime menus, but at much more reasonable prices. A good Italian eatery near us charges $5.50 for soup or salad and lasagna at lunch. After 5 P.M. the owners light the candles and double the prices for the exact same meal. If you eat lunch instead of dinner at this restaurant just once a week, by the end of the year you will save $250—and that's a lot of lasagna.

31. Keep your popcorn in top condition.

Popcorn is a favorite treat for frugal snackers, because it's cheap, healthful, and easy to prepare. But if you get a bad batch, unpopped kernels can cut down on your enjoyment and your sav-

Don't bother buying those expensive little plastic "peanuts" for packing material when you're sending breakables through the mail. Pop up a few batches of popcorn (without butter, naturally) and use that instead. Popcorn works just as effectively in cushioning your present, is much kinder on the environment, and at 60 cents for a 6-ounce bag is one-fourth the price of a bag of packing pellets. Recipients of your package can empty the popcorn onto their lawn and give a treat to the birds and squirrels instead of wondering what the heck to do with all those Styrofoam peanuts.

ings. Try this trick: Keep your popcorn in the fridge. Some people swear that popcorn pops better if you do this.

32. Is a whole chicken really the better buy?

Not always. About one-third of that bird will be wasted as bones and cartilage. If you use them to make stock, the whole chicken is a good buy, but if your family is picky and likes only white meat or legs, suddenly the whole bird doesn't look like such a big deal. In our local stores boned breasts regularly go on sale for $1.99; a whole chicken would have to sell for under 66 cents a pound to beat that price.

33. Make use of extra apples.

Here's a thrifty, time-tested kitchen tip that worked for our grandmothers. Are you tired of buying brown sugar for baking, only to find it turns rock hard and useless by the time you're ready to use it? Try adding an apple to the brown sugar bag to keep the sugar moist for weeks. (An apple placed in a bag of potatoes also keeps the potatoes fresh and prevents sprouting.) Now you know what to do with the rest of that large bag of apples you lugged home from the farmer's market or supermarket.

34. Use it twice for half the price.

Come November, just about every doorway in our neighborhood is littered with the rotting remains of once-proud Halloween pumpkins. What can you do with your jack-o'-lantern once its trick-and-treating days are over? Well, if your child doesn't object too much, you can resurrect it as a homemade pumpkin pie or quick bread just in time for Thanksgiving. If the pumpkin was carved recently and is not beginning to spoil, you can cut it into chunks and boil or steam it for about 25 minutes in a saucepan with a little water. Then cut the pulp from the skin and mash it with a fork or potato masher and use it in your favorite pumpkin pie (or muffin or quick-bread) recipe.

35. Who needs this?

Tupperware containers can be pretty pricey, especially for those color-coordinated sets; many small sets sell for $20. We've found that cottage cheese, cheese spread, and ricotta containers (thoroughly washed, of course) work just as well for storing extra food in the refrigerator and the freezer. Tubs of soft margarine also last forever and can be successfully cleaned in the dishwasher. The only tricky part is identifying which container holds its advertised product and which is currently in use for leftovers!

36. Smart buys save money.

Throw away your paper coffee filters and purchase one of those new gold metal coffee filters for $20. Since paper filters cost $2.50 or more for a package of 40, your payback time for the metal filter is well under a year. Plus you won't have to worry about bleach from the paper filters leaching into your java.

37. Make your own herb vinegar.

It's soooo easy. Use fresh basil, thyme, tarragon, or rosemary from your garden or from the produce section of a fine supermarket. Place the herbs in a bottle of wine vinegar or apple cider vinegar (leftover wine works well too) in a ratio of 4 tablespoons herbs to 4 cups vinegar. Cap or cork (be sure not to use a metal cap) and let the mixture sit for a month. Then strain out the herbs and pour the vinegar into a clean bottle, along with one or two of the herb sprigs for a nice visual effect. You now have expensive herb vinegar (usually over $3 a bottle) for the price of plain vinegar (under $1 a bottle). If you use leftover wine and herbs from your own garden, this homemade vinegar is practically free.

> **P**retty up your bottle with a ribbon and a handwritten label, and you have a great gourmet gift that cost you only pennies.

Making the Most of Your Clothing Budget

38. Rent like the gents.

Going to a wedding, formal dinner, or an opera benefit? Don't rush out and spend hundreds on a dress you'll wear once—rent it instead. Men have done this for years with their tuxedos, and now most major cities have similar formal rental services for women. If you can't find such a place, buy a dress at one of those upscale resale shops that accepts clothing from clients to sell on consignment. Wear your purchase once, clean it, and then return it to the shop to sell for you. The usual profit split is 50/50.

39. Steer clear of dry cleaners.

Even if you buy wisely, the hidden costs of clothes—such as maintaining them—may wipe out all your savings. When shopping, try to purchase garments you can launder in the washer or at least hand wash, because dry cleaning is very, very expensive. In fact, our local dry cleaning establishment charges more to clean a silk blouse ($3.75) than the cost of buying one at the consignment shop around the corner ($3.00).

40. Wean your teens off impulse buying.

Give your older teens a budget and their own purchasing power to avoid getting caught in the trap of subsidizing their gotta-have-it fashion habits. By budgeting, you'll help keep spending under

If you buy a small plastic or wooden laundry drying rack that will fit in your tub, you'll find it easier to do your fine laundry by hand. Your clothes also will last much longer that way, since the harsh chemicals dry cleaners use will destroy them over time. Don't automatically assume that you need to hand wash everything, though. We've successfully washed lingerie, sweaters, nylons, and even slipcovers in the washing machine using cold water and the delicate cycle. And remember, cashmere—one of the most luxurious woolens—is actually supposed to be washed in the machine!

control and cut down on impulse purchases. For example, say they're given $250 for new fall clothes for school. They can spend $150 on sneakers and buy the rest of their wardrobe in the resale shop (or make do with last year's stuff), or allocate their funds more wisely. The important thing is to stick with the budget and not criticize their choices—after all, they're the ones who have to live with them.

41. Drag your feet.

Persuade your schoolchildren not to buy *all* their back-to-school clothing before school begins. A few weeks later, your kids will have a better idea of what "everyone" is wearing this year. While you may be appalled that young children are already slaves to fashion, it does make sense to buy the type of clothes your child will wear instead of having a whole season's worth of clothes hanging unworn in the closet. If you hold back about 25 percent of the clothing budget, your kids will have some money left to go out and buy those must-have clothes in October without going into debt.

42. Consider becoming a FRUMP.

That's a Frugal, Responsible, Unpretentious, Mature Person (man or woman) who ignores the latest ridiculous fashions and prefers to wear old and comfortable clothes, such as white shirts and a favorite pair of trousers. Barbara Hovanetz coined this memorable term in her book *Auntie Barbara's Tips for an Ordinary Life.*

It's possible to look great and stylish with nothing but two pairs of jeans, a pair of sneakers, and two shirts. You can buy the jeans (both colored and blue denim) and two classic, mostly cotton shirts at the Gap for just $30 to $40 apiece. For under $200, you'll get clothes that will last for years and won't go out of style. Or you can blow the same amount on one trendy vest that a year from now you'll be embarrassed even to admit you bought, let alone wore. Which would you rather do?

43. Be skeptical about sales.

They're not always money-savers—especially if they lead you to buy something you don't need. Because you've found some "great deals," you can "save money all the way to the poorhouse" (as Martha's father used to say).

> Clothing stores are notorious for using grouped special sales to get you to buy more than you want. The most common ploy is "Buy 3, Get 1 Free," which is fine if you need three of an item, but usually you want only one. You can make the most of this type of sale if you are lucky enough to have a friend or relative who shares your taste and is the same size. If so, you can bring that person shopping with you and split the savings. If not, shop at another store that offers low prices all the time, not just during sales.

44. Get double duty for your dollars.

There's no need to buy tailor's chalk to mark darts and hems on your sewing projects—use slivers of soap. The soap marking will wash away completely the first time you launder the garment.

45. Make it last longer.

Quality leather boots and shoes are usually a good investment, but if you live in an area where the roads and sidewalks are salted in winter, your investment can be ruined by salt residue. Remove salt stains quickly by wiping the leather with a mixture of half white vinegar and half water. Then wipe with a leather conditioner or polish. Your boots and shoes will look better and last longer.

46. Don't drop beaucoup dollars on designer clothes just for their labels.

Very often the garments and accessories are made by Asian third-party manufacturers, anyway. But if you really love a designer's work and must buy something, look for outlet locations. Outlets usually are located close to large metropolitan areas or vacation

Liz Claiborne, Anne Klein, Calvin Klein, and Ralph Lauren all have outlets in Kittery, Maine, and Williamsburg, Virginia. Calvin Klein, Liz Claiborne, and Ralph Lauren also have outlets in Foley, Alabama. Lauren, who must take his Western thing very seriously, also has outlets in Rapid City, South Dakota, Billings, Montana, and Jackson, Wyoming. In addition, the largest outlet mall in the United States was recently built in Gurnee, Illinois. Fortunately for smart shoppers, the trend toward outlet discount stores is growing rapidly. Check out *The Outlet Shopper's Guide* (Lazar Media Group, $9.95) to find the ones nearest you.

What kinds of savings can you find? Recently a pair of Calvin Klein jeans listed at $56.99 was selling for $39.99, and a $380 blazer was going for $204.99 at one of the Calvin Klein outlets. Liz Claiborne claims its outlet store prices are usually 30 percent off department store prices.

Keep tissue paper in all your shoes, and store your shoes in their boxes. They won't get wrinkly or scuffed as quickly and will look good for ages.

spots. Let's face it, if your holiday shopping choices are between a shiny polyester T-shirt that says something like "I Ate Bear Mountain" versus a Calvin Klein sweater, well, you gotta go for the sweater.

47. Who needs this?

Why pay $20 or more for expensive boot trees when a tube of rolled-up newspaper works just as well? The tube not only lengthens the life of your boots by keeping them from cracking at the ankles, but also helps wet boots dry out faster and more evenly by improving air circulation.

48. Shop resale or garage sales.

Resale shops have one big advantage over garage sales, since most resale shops offer you return privileges within a few days of your purchase if your clothes don't fit or if your kids reject them. If you feel awkward shopping resale for your own clothes, next Halloween cozy up to the idea with an initial foray into the land of Goodwill and Salvation Army (or specialized children's resale shops) in search of costume materials for the kids. Before you know it you'll be happily shopping for yourself too. Darcie's latest find was a fawn-colored Anne Klein silk suit for $30.

Think of it as an exciting treasure hunt. As the slogan for one off-price clothing store puts it, "Whoever gets the best deals wins!"

49. Raid your own closets.

While you're at it, don't forget to take those old bridesmaid's dresses hanging in your closet to the resale shop as well. Or cut off some of the excess length and rehem to make perfect formal dress-up clothes or Halloween outfits for your school-age children.

50. From here to maternity.

Resale shops featuring maternity clothes are just beginning to spring up in many large cities—thank goodness. Most maternity garments can be kindly described as functional in appearance. (If you're not feeling kind, you could rant and rave about why the mother-to-be needs to be covered with little duckies and teddies all over her clothes, since she's carrying a baby, not becoming one!) You certainly don't want these shapeless clothes hanging in your closet once the need for them is over. Buying maternity clothes at resale shops makes perfect sense. Since the clothes aren't worn very long, they usually are in great condition. Some of the new maternity consignment stores even rent glitzy dresses for those special events. If you don't have a resale store in your community, see if you can swap items with friends—if they're kind enough to schedule their pregnancies around yours.

We called our local maternity resale shop to check prices, and found that they sell manufacturers' samples and overstocks as well as clothes for resale. This store is representative of other resale shops in offering discounts ranging from 30 percent to 70 percent of retail prices.

> **D**on't overlook your husband's closet. He may have the perfect-size sweats, winter coat, and bathrobe you need as you approach the end of your pregnancy. You've already given up a lot for this baby, so he can give up a few items of clothing temporarily, don't you think?

Here's what to do if you have a drawer full of nylons with one good leg and one bad: Cut off the bad right leg of one pair and the bad left leg of another pair. Then put one pair on over the other and voilà! a complete set! If this trick saves you replacing just one pair a week, by the end of the year you will have saved over $125.

51. Get a leg up on panty hose costs.

If you have to wear panty hose to work, you're suffering enough without having to spend $15 to $20 a month buying the darned things. (One study we've come across recently claims that "the average woman tears her panty hose three times a week"!) A good source for new and slightly irregular nylons is the L'eggs and Hanes outlet catalog. Depending on how many pairs you order, you can get 50 to 60 percent off the retail cost. This catalog also has inexpensive sweats and tights for women and girls as well as bras and underwear. Call 910-744-1170 for a free catalog.

52. Who needs this?

Don't buy delicate lingerie wash bags (priced at $24 for three small bags). Instead, just throw your nylons and other fine washables into a pillowcase and wash them on your washing machine's delicate setting. It works beautifully. While you're at it, throw all your family's socks (especially those teeny baby booties) into a pillowcase so you don't have to worry about stray socks getting gobbled up mysteriously during the washing process.

53. Blend in.

Another way to avoid dry cleaning costs is never, ever to buy 100 percent cotton dress shirts. Sure, they look great when crisply pressed—but do you want to slave over a hot ironing board every time you wash them? We like to buy shirts in 60 percent cotton,

40 percent polyester blends. (Make sure the polyester content does not exceed 50 percent, or the shirt may begin to look too cheap and shiny after several washings.) The blended-fabric shirts come out of the dryer without those thousands of tiny wrinkles endemic to all-cotton shirts, and they look just fine without any pressing (especially if you hang them and button them right up to the collar while they're still warm). You might as well reap some of the benefits of modern chemistry by buying no-iron clothes—and if you buy good-quality shirts, you won't have to worry about looking like you're going to a disco.

54. A saline solution.

Instead of going through a bottle of color-safe bleach each week or two, just add two pinches of table salt to your laundry to keep colors bright. This works especially well for cleaning your kids' heavily soiled, formerly colorful gym shoes.

If you wash canvas shoes in a pillowcase, the shoes will stay new-looking longer. This tip only works with young children, though, who don't yet *want* their shoes to look beat-up and scruffy.

55. Toe the line on new shoes.

For just $3—one-tenth the cost of an average pair of shoes—you can get twice the life out of your footgear simply by having a cobbler add rubber toe and heel taps.

56. Don't junk those hole-y sweaters.

You can buy suede elbow patches, available in a whole range of coordinating colors, at any sewing store. They take just minutes to sew on—and they'll even make you look distinguished and professorial when you wear them. Not bad for $3!

Inspiration for Better, Longer-lasting, and Cheaper Transportation

57. A homemade car emergency kit makes good, safe sense.

Many stores and auto supply houses carry preassembled emergency kits containing items such as jumper cables, siphon hose, fire extinguisher, spotlight, hammer, Fix-A-Flat, and some first-aid items. They usually sell for over $50. You can customize one yourself—you probably have some of these items already at home—for about half the price, especially if you use an old briefcase or carry-on bag to hold it. (We like to throw in emergency rations, such as a box of raisins, and a few bungee cords too.)

58. Give your brakes a break.

The average cost of a brake job on a domestic car is $89.95. If you brake slowly and try to avoid sudden stops, you will save hundreds of dollars in brake jobs over the life of your car, while saving gas and reducing the potential for having an accident.

59. Get the most money for your old car.

When you eventually buy a new car, sell your old one yourself—nine times out of ten you'll get more money for it than from the dealer.

Start by giving your car a thorough vacuuming, wash and wax—and apply a protectant, such as Armor All, to the dashboard for good measure. Then remove all those old Reagan/Bush or Mondale/Ferraro bumper stickers. (Use a hair dryer to soften the glue.) As an additional benefit, once you do all this, you might like your "new" clean car enough to keep it! If you do decide to sell it, make sure your automotive log of maintenance and repairs is fully up to date. This will help buyers see that you took care of your car. Finally, know what your car is worth and price it realistically. Your public library probably has the same books the dealers use (look for *The Blue Book* or *The NADA [National Auto Dealer's Association] Guide*). If not, check your bookstore.

Here's one example of the money you can save by selling your car yourself. A 1987 Volkswagen GTI in good condition will bring you around $3,875 if you trade it in to a dealer, who will then list the car for $5,250 or so (the retail cost for this particular used car). Or you could advertise this car for $5,000 and sell it privately for around $4,800, which is $1,000 more than you'd get from your dealer.

60. Another freebie.

Brag to your coworkers and friends about how well you maintain your car. When it comes time to sell it, you won't have to spend a penny on advertising, because word-of-mouth will do it for you. If your car's reputation speaks for itself, you can save $60 by not taking out a small for-sale ad in your metropolitan newspaper for a few weeks, as most private car sellers do.

61. Cut back to one car.

If you are a two-car family but live in an area with public transportation, consider getting rid of one vehicle and using buses, trains, cabs, or ride sharing, instead. All of those costs together will not add up to what a second car costs you in maintenance, gas, plates, parking fees, city stickers, and insurance. For example, many people own a second car that they drive to the train station every work day. If they would take a cab to the station instead, they'd spend around $6 a day, or $1,500 per year. This option makes a lot of sense when you consider that auto insurance alone is probably close to $1,500.

62. Can the car entirely.

Use public transportation and hired cars for all your travel needs. This is particularly appropriate for one-car families who use their car infrequently (such as city dwellers who use the vehicle primarily for weekend jaunts and shopping). If you need a car for an occasional weekend trip, shop around for a competitive rental rate. (You might be able to get good rental deals through your credit card or frequent flyer affiliations. If not, check the less well known rental companies instead of starting with the biggest names.) As an added bonus, the rental cars come insured in many states (read the fine print), so that is another expenditure you may avoid.

63. Another freebie.

Check the air in your tires regularly. This simple procedure can extend the life of your car and cut your operating costs. Underinflated tires are one of the most common causes of premature tire wear, poor handling, and high fuel consumption. New car tires cost between $50 and $100 each, depending on the model of car and its wheel size. So maintaining the tires you already have instead of needing to buy new ones can save you $200 to $400. Refer to your owner's manual for proper inflation pressures. If you don't feel comfortable checking the pressure yourself, ask a gas station attendant to show you how.

64. Make a collision revision.

If your car is proudly referred to as "the old war-horse" and already sports some honorable scars from stone chips and parking lot dings, consider dropping the collision portion of your insurance. If the resale value of your car is under $2,000, you don't have to consider this option—just do it. Collision coverage with a $200 deductible runs around $120 every six months, so you'll save nearly $250 a year just by making this one small change in your auto insurance.

65. Use it twice for half the price.

Reuse old, soft, all-cotton cloth diapers as car polishing cloths—they take off the wax beautifully and don't scratch the paint. Old bath towels also work well. You can save up to $15 each time you take this advice instead of heading to the store and buying a pack of polishing cloths or a chamois leather.

66. Another freebie.

Combine something you have to do—commuting—with something you enjoy doing—bicycling. Give biking to work a try if you like to bike on weekends and if you live within ten miles of your office. It's not something you have to do every day, but after a while you may find that you miss your morning bike ride if the weather makes it impossible to ride that day. If you haven't tried riding a bike lately, you'll be surprised at how much better (and more fun to ride) today's mountain bikes are than your old Schwinn. Since a train pass can cost $45 a month for an under-ten-mile commute, this option is well worth considering. Remember that you won't need to pay any parking fees—or take out a health club membership, for that matter!

67. "Nearly" new can mean savings for you.

If you're looking for a new car, keep your eyes open for good deals on nearly new cars (especially test-drive models or dealer-driven cars) that still have a warranty. To achieve this goal you need to scour the automotive want ads daily and act quickly when you see a closeout price on a car you like. Martha's family has bought cars this way twice, and each time saved 20 to 30 percent off the list price on a less than one-year-old car with under 10,000 miles, in great condition.

68. Compare insurance costs.

When trying to decide which car to buy, first call your insurance agent to find out the approximate insurance cost. Some models may have significantly higher costs than cars in the same class because of their accident, repair, and theft rates. For example, Camaros and Firebirds are very expensive to insure due to their high theft and accident rates, and VW Golfs and Jettas are vulnerable to car radio thefts. On the other hand, Ford Tauruses, Honda Accords, Toyota Camrys, and most Volvos are reasonably inexpensive to insure because of their low theft and accident rates. Of these three, Tauruses are the least expensive to insure, followed by Accords and Camrys. If you're torn between two similar cars, knowing the insurance cost can be the deciding factor in your buying decision.

69. Who needs this?

Don't ever spend big bucks on having your car rustproofed. New cars' paint jobs and built-in rustproofing have improved dramatically in the last five years. General Motors cars, for example, now come with two-sided galvanized steel bodies that naturally resist rust. And Saturn cars and some minivans have plastic body panels that don't rust at all. Even if you live in a snowy area, a $300 rustproofing job seems ridiculously expensive compared to the $10 per year it will cost you simply to hose off the undercarriage yourself. At that rate, your professional rustproofing has a payback period of thirty years—in other words, you'll still be paying for it long after the car is gone.

70. Learn how to change the oil in your car yourself.

An oil change will run you about $10 if you do it yourself—so you'll save about $20 each oil change by avoiding Jiffy Lube

(Since your car's oil should be changed four times a year, you can save about $80 annually by doing the job at home.) If you neglect regular oil changes, an engine rebuild costs *at least* $1,000—so don't procrastinate! This step-by-step guide will give you the overview. Then look in your car's manual for specific instructions and how much oil you'll need to add for each oil change.

1. Check that you can reach the filter and drain plug. (See your owner's manual for details.) Some cars' engines are much trickier to work on than others.

2. Buy oil and a good-quality filter. Rather than buy the filter from your dealer, which can be quite expensive, look for Fram filters at Trak Auto and other auto supply stores. Try to get them on sale, of course, and stock up. If you know the year, make, and model of your car, a sales clerk can tell you what filter you'll need.

3. You'll need something to catch the old oil in. You can buy a jerry can with a bung hole in the side that doubles as a drain pan and carrying can. You'll also need an oil filter wrench and a socket of the right size for your drain plug. (Check your manual again.)

4. Make sure you can remove the old oil filter—it may be tight. Then drive your car for a little while, come home, and drain the oil while the engine's still warm. Remove the old filter, making sure not to leave its gasket on the engine. Install the new filter according to the manual's directions. Reinstall the drain plug.

5. Fill 'er up with fresh oil. Then start the engine, check for leaks, and you're done. (Recycle your used oil by bringing it to a gas station or to some community recycling centers.)

71. Visit your local dump or salvage yard.

Why buy new parts if you own a six-year-old, 60,000-mile car? When your car is misbehaving and your dealer is quoting astronomical rates for replacement parts (not to mention the labor), scrounging around your local junkyard can be a very profitable way to spend a Saturday morning. Having some technical knowledge helps, though, because one automotive part can look very like all the others on the shelf. If you don't want other mechanical problems down the road, it's imperative that you find the right part to fit your car.

We called our local auto wreckers and priced some Ford Taurus parts. We were quoted $35 for a steel wheel, $500 for a door, and $550 for an entire transmission. In contrast, the Ford dealer in town is charging $61 for a wheel, $600 for a door, and between $1,000 to $3,000 for a transmission.

> **O**r you can try J.C. Whitney & Co.'s enormous catalog of automotive parts and accessories for almost every model of car on the road today. Call them at 312-431-6102 before paying dealer prices.

72. Who needs this?

Never buy an extended-service contract from a car dealer. The service contract can cost between $600 to $2,000 for two to five years of coverage, but tends to expire just as the car is starting to need repairs—and often the original warranty covers you for most of that period anyway. These contracts are a major source of commissions for car salespeople, which is why they push them so aggressively. (The same holds true for buying extended warranties on major appliances and electronic equipment.) In fact, according to major retailers, only 12 to 20 percent of people who buy extended warranties ever use them. Instead of paying several hundred dollars on a warranty, then, it's smarter to start a just-in-case savings account instead. If you don't need the money for repairs, you'll be able to use it down the road when it's time to buy a replacement model.

73. Consider leasing.

If you're hung up on always having a new car, a lease may make sense for you. (Of course, true frugal fanatics prefer driving their vehicles into the ground.) Occasionally car manufacturers offer subsidized promotional leases on models they want to move out of the showroom. Look for newspaper ads in your paper's automotive section announcing this kind of lease deal. When you take out a lease, remember that you're not paying for an entire car. You're paying only for the portion of the car you use, so you can invest most of your capital instead of tying it up in a car purchase. (Cadillac and Ford have recently announced that they are offering favorable leases on some *used* cars, which will make leasing even more affordable.)

Road & Track magazine lists these reasons to lease:

- Monthly payments will be lower than if you had bought the car with a loan.
- You can lease a more expensive car than you'd be able to afford if you took out a loan.
- A minimal down payment is required, usually just the first month's payment and a refundable security deposit.
- The car will be covered by its new car warranty during the entire time you own it, so you won't have to pay for any repairs.
- You can let the dealer worry about reselling it after your lease is over.

A typical lease lasts two to four years. At the end of the lease, you turn the car in and lease another car—or you may have the option to buy the car you've been driving.

There are several caveats, though. By leasing, you never build up equity in your car. If you want to buy a car next time, you'll have to get your down payment from your savings instead of by selling or trading in your current car. You also must take good care of the car you lease. If you exceed the amount of mileage the lease allows you—typically around 15,000 miles a year—you'll get zinged with penalty charges at the end of the lease. You'll also have your security deposit docked if the car is not maintained properly or is damaged in any way. And you'll incur large penalties if you back out of the lease early. So this option is not for everyone—let the leaser beware!

74. Always bargain when purchasing a car.

Here are a few simple negotiating techniques that can really work. First, decide what type of car you're looking for and shop around to see which models will fit the bill. Don't set your heart on one car or one color. The more flexible you can be, the more likely you are to come up with a good deal. Then make sure you know the dealer's cost on the models you're most interested in (by reading *Consumer Reports* or consulting *The Blue Book* at your library). Once you know what the dealer paid for the car, you can add what you think is a fair profit for the dealer and then make your offer.

On the other hand, know how much you can afford and don't budge or give into temptation on adding options you don't need. Be willing to walk away from a dealer who will not give you what you want. Patience definitely pays off. It may take a few trips to several different dealers and a few months scouring the classified ads before you find the right car—and the best deal—so start looking well before your current car gives up the ghost. Rather than visit every dealer in town, though, you might want to choose the two or three closest to you and announce that you're looking for a certain type of car and that you're planning to visit the two other local dealers in your search for the right price. Being firm about your needs and clear on your intentions can convince a dealer that you're serious, and encourage him or her to meet you halfway.

75. Join the club.

If you're not confident about your own negotiating skills, consider joining the American Automobile Association. Some AAA chapters offer a free car-buying service for their members, in which they act as brokers and negotiate the best price for you on the car you've selected. Call the AAA (check your phone book for the nearest affiliate) to find out if you're lucky enough to have this service in your area.

76. Shop at the right time.

August can be a very good time to buy a new car since the new models are delivered in September. Dealers often have special incentives to sell their current inventory, and you'll avoid any price increases that inevitably come along with the brand-new models.

You can still practice good timing even if it's not August. Try the end of the month—that's when salespeople are most anxious about making quotas or qualifying for bonuses.

77. Don't expect a "deal" from your dealer.

When it comes to financing your car purchase, don't automatically opt for dealer financing. Often credit unions are your best bet. A recent national survey of banks, savings and loans, and credit unions found that most credit unions charge a full percentage point less interest than banks—and 1¼ points less than savings and loans on new car loans. We found that our local credit union offers a 6.5 percent interest rate on three-year loan for a new car and a 7.9 percent rate on a three-year loan for a used car

The AAA's Chicago Motor Club also publishes a free checklist of what to look for when shopping for a car. You can send a self-addressed stamped envelope to: Car Buying Checklist, AAA-Chicago Motor Club, Public Affairs Department, 999 E. Touhy Avenue, Des Plaines, IL 60018, or call 708-390-9000.

purchase. Our bank had a 7 percent rate for a three-year new car loan and 9.25 percent for a three-year used car loan. The community Ford dealer was surprisingly competitive on a new Taurus—it offered a subsidized rate of 6.9 percent for a four-year loan. But the dealer's used car rate varied from 10 percent to a whopping 18 percent, depending on your credit rating.

Another smart option is to take out a home equity loan to buy a new car. This may be the cheapest possible type of car financing, because you currently can get very low interest rates, *and* the interest you pay is tax deductible, unlike a conventional car loan. At this writing, home equity loan interest rates were under 10 percent. This rate is favorable if you're buying a used car, compared to the other financing alternatives just discussed.

78. Get a rebate without a recall.

Are you due a rebate for the repair work done on your car? Maybe. . . . If it's been more than a year since you bought your car, if you've changed your address or purchased a used car, the manufacturer's recall notice may never reach you through the mail. In addition, manufacturers often issue special service alerts to dealers about persistent problems that haven't reached the recall stage yet still may be eligible for "customer satisfaction" rebates. While the mechanic is tearing apart your transmission,

Need help comparing new car financing costs? A handy table developed by William Bryan, director of the Bureau of Economic and Business Research at the University of Illinois, will help you choose between a manufacturer's rebate and cut-rate financing when you're buying a new car. Best of all, it's free. Send a self-addressed stamped envelope to Rebate Table, *Kiplinger's Personal Finance,* 1729 H Street NW, Washington, DC 20006.

have the garage manager run a computer inquiry checking for recall or reimbursement programs related to your make and model. We know of one man who had his entire bill of $411 rebated by General Motors after he insisted on a recall inquiry.

79. Compare clones.

There's often a big price difference in the same car if it is sold under different names. For instance, Chevrolet and Suzuki both sell the same four-wheel-drive vehicle, but it will cost you less to buy the Geo Tracker. (Suzuki calls it the Sidekick.) Another Chevrolet car, the Geo Prizm, will cost you over $1,000 more if you buy it under its Toyota Corolla nameplate.

If your car has persistent problems and your mechanic can't or won't make an inquiry, or if you just want to satisfy yourself, contact the National Highway Traffic Safety Administration's Technical Reference Division (202-366-2768) to see if your car is the subject of a special service bulletin. The call isn't free, but your peace of mind—or rebate!—may be worth it.

Making Your Garden Work for You

80. Grow your own.

Gardening does take some effort, especially the first year when you are making your beds. But having a productive vegetable garden doesn't take any special skills, and even a limited amount of home-grown veggies can have a terrific impact on your food budget. For example, Darcie likes to grow her own snow peas, which cost $1.50 for 8 ounces in the store. Last year her $2 investment in seeds gave her fresh peas all spring and fall, plus a freezerful of frozen ones too. Since she cooks Oriental-style quite often and uses a lot of peas, we estimate that growing the peas saved her $75 this year. Between growing tomatoes, cukes, zucchini, beans (fresh and for soup), carrots, dill, cilantro, strawberries, and peppers, Darcie slashes about $675 from her family's food budget every year.

81. Make your own stakes.

Tired of seeing the grocery money your garden saves you being eaten up by exorbitant prices for bean posts and pea fences? Grow your own for pennies! Corn and yucca stalks make strong and attractive stakes for a variety of climbing plants, such as cucumbers, tomatoes, beans, and peas.

Saving over $600 a year with dirt and seeds sounds great. Now let's see what "growing your own" adds up to over time. Assume you invest these savings in a conservative mutual fund paying 6 percent interest. At the end of five years of vegetable gardening you will have saved over $4,000. That's an impressive profit from a simple patch of veggies.

82. Another freebie.

Make your own hot caps for your tomatoes, peppers, and other heat-loving plants to keep them alive during colder weather. You can recycle old grocery bags with this simple method: Cut a hole in the bottom of the bag and place it over the plant, anchoring the bottom of the bag with small rocks or bricks. Fold the top over a few times to close the bag during a frost. Open it when the weather warms up. These bags also help discourage pests and can be left on the whole season to decompose naturally. Or you can cut the bottom off gallon water and milk jugs and use them to get an early start on the growing season.

83. Use it twice for half the price.

For smaller plants, use old coffee filters for hot caps. They let in light and air and retain heat, just like expensive landscape fabrics. Anchor them around seedlings with clothespins or rocks. Old newspapers (black-and-white sections only, please) work well too. Meanwhile, a package of ten flimsy waxed paper hot caps at your local garden supply store costs around $2.50, or 25 cents for each plant you need to cover. If you have a large garden, these costs will mount up in a hurry.

84. Be your own lawn service.

Having your grass cut weekly by someone else just doesn't make sense, especially when your lawn may need attention twice a week in the spring and only once every two weeks or so in August and September. Just a cut alone, exclusive of edging and cultivating, can cost $25 or more. Unless your property is very large, a 22-inch hand mower is probably all you need to get the job done in an hour or less. Assuming twenty cuts a season, your service could be costing you $500 or more a year. For real fuel savings plus an exercise benefit, use an old-fashioned (and wonderfully quiet!) push-reel model.

85. Is it more frugal to rent or buy?

Take a minute to figure it out for yourself, because if you don't you could easily spend an entire year's food budget on labor-saving gardening tools. Sometimes it's more economical to rent seldom-used equipment rather than to shell out major dollars for an item that will sit around the garage taking up space 364 days a year. For example, a Rototiller from Gardener's Supply in Burlington, Vermont (1-802-863-1700), costs $259. Renting one from your local Rent Anything for a couple of hours to get your garden in shape for spring planting costs around $40. Split the rental costs with a neighbor, and it works out to a very long thirteen-year payback for purchasing a Rototiller. Your model will probably be out of date and costing you maintenance money by then.

86. Wring every last drop out of your water.

If you live in the Southwest, or anywhere else where water rates are high, you probably already monitor your garden's consumption of water like a hawk. An entirely porous soaker hose, such as the Moisture Master made by Aquapore of Phoenix, Arizona (1-800-635-8379), distributes water directly and evenly into the soil, so that almost none is lost to evaporation. As a result, you may use up to 70 percent less water in your garden—and thereby cut your water bill by the same amount. An added plus—the Moisture Master is made from recycled tires.

87. Become a rose rustler.

Start or extend your garden by acquiring plants through cuttings rather than purchasing. Is it worth the effort? You bet. Rosebushes routinely cost $10 to $15 apiece. Ask neighborhood gardeners if you can take a slip (a great way to make new friends or just get a tour of a garden you admire). Or buy one bush and propagate a whole hedge. Warning—this method only works with own-root roses. Many hybrid teas, which are grafted onto a foreign, more hardy root stock, will not come true with this method.

Here's how to take a rose cutting. Snip off a young cane no thicker than a pencil. Let it stand overnight in a jar of water, to which chopped willow twigs (which contain the root stimulant rhizocaline) have been added. Next day remove all the leaves on the lower half of your cutting and plant the cutting in a pot containing a 50/50 mixture of peat and sand. Water until damp, not wet, and place the pot in a clear plastic bag. Leave the bagged pot in a low-light east or north window. Your cutting should be rooted and ready to come out of the bag in three weeks. If you don't have access to willow twigs, you can purchase a commercial rooting powder from a reputable garden supply company, such as Mellinger's (1-800-321-7444).

88. Who needs this?

Instead of paying a lawn service to come several times a year to spray chemicals on your lawn, you can buy weed repellents yourself and spread them over the grass at a fraction of the cost. Chemlawn charges $42 an application for an average 5,000-square-foot lawn and recommends four to six applications annually. You can save up to $222 every year by buying a couple of $15 bags of Scott's Turfbuilder weedkiller and fertilizer. Or you can buy a few packets of perennial seeds for less than $5, convince your neighbors that the prairie or woodland look is best in this ecologically aware decade, and spend a year hand-weeding your yard until the wildflowers take hold.

89. Use it twice for half the price.

Instead of paying $7 a packet for garden ties, section old panty hose to use for garden ties for tomatoes, hollyhocks, and other tall plants that tend to fall over. These nylon bands are good for bundling newspapers for recycling as well.

> The panty part of old panty hose makes a great filter for shop vacs. Tie a knot in each leg near the crotch and trim off excess below the knot; then fasten the panty part over the vac exhaust with a rubber band or tape.

90. Plant desert blooms.

If you live in an area where water is expensive, landscape with arid-land plants such as mesquite, desert willow, ocotillo, ironwood, sweet acacia, blue paloverde, creosote, banana yucca, autumn sage, and Mexican elderberry. Your water bills will drop dramatically if you don't have to dump gallons on your landscape every day to maintain exotic plants in a climate for which they never were intended.

91. Make it last longer.

Good-quality yard and garden tools are worth the investment only if you keep them in good repair. Here's an easy way to clean and lubricate digging tools: Fill a five-gallon can with sand. Add the old motor oil drained from your car or lawn mower. Keep this can in the garage or shed or wherever you store your tools. Whenever you use a digging tool, plunge it into the can several times after each use. The blade will be cleaned and lubricated.

92. Slug the bugs.

Don't lose your home-grown veggies to an onslaught of slugs. Recycle old cans, jars, and lidless plastic containers as slug traps in the garden. Dig a hole the size of the container and sink the trap with the top flush to the ground. Fill the traps with salty or soapy water and bait the rims with fermenting bread dough or thin slices of potato.

> Leftover beer gone flat in the bottle? Beer is one of the best baits you can use in a garden slug trap—plus it does double duty as the drowning medium too. At least they die happy.

93. Build your own bug traps.

Pest traps can cost $25, but you can catch your own yellow jackets, wasps, or flies with a properly prepared old plastic milk jug container. Cut an opening large enough to fit your hand through in one of the panels opposite the handle. Mix up a bait solution of ½ cup vinegar, ½ cup water, and 2 tablespoons molasses. Pour this mixture into the bottom of the jug and hang the jug by the handle in a tree or from a fence post. Experiment with different bait media (try yeast or small amounts of rotted meat) to catch a wider variety of pests. But remember—don't hang the traps near the plants the pests eat, or the bait will draw them right to your flowers and veggies.

94. Make it last longer.

Garden hoses are expensive (good ones cost well over $20 for a 50-foot section), so don't shorten the life of yours unnecessarily by storing it improperly on a nail or peg. Inevitably the hose will kink and sag, which will lead to cracked rubber and eventual hose failure. Hang your hoses properly in wide loops on an inexpensive rack or, better yet, recycle an old tire rim to make a rack for free.

95. Another freebie.

Instead of buying fertilizer for houseplants, put a barrel out in your garden to collect rainwater and use that to water your indoor plants. They'll thrive without your having to use any artificial chemicals—and you'll save $10 each time you forgo buying plant food.

96. Use it twice for half the price.

Fertilize your roses and evergreens with used coffee grounds instead of buying acidifying plant food for $6 a jar. You can dump the grounds you *didn't* put down your sink into the garden. (Banana peels also are useful soil enrichers for your roses.)

97. Spice and easy.

Ounce for ounce, herbs and teas are some of the most expensive items on supermarket shelves. If you have two square feet of garden space (which can include a shelf on your kitchen window), you can grow enough basil, mint, parsley, cilantro, and chamomile to keep a family of four flush in spices and tea all year round. Fresh herbs are hardy perennials, they thrive in a sunny corner of your yard or a window box, and they need little attention.

If you enjoy chives with your bagels in the morning, as we do, bland-tasting dried chives cost as much as $3.09 for a tiny .012-ounce jar at the grocery store. If you go through two small jars a month, that's $74.16 a year just for chives. If you plant your own for an initial investment of $1 to $2 a plant, you'll have all the chives you'll ever need for years to come, because they're self-seeding and pop up like clockwork every spring. The same goes for oregano and mint, which grow so rapidly and vibrantly they may threaten to take over your garden.

98. Dry herbs to last throughout the year.

Air-drying gives the best flavor and doesn't take long. These step-by-step guidelines come from Drusilla Banks, home economics advisor for the Cooperative Extension service of the University of Illinois.

Herbs are ready to harvest when they begin to flower. For best results, harvest them early in the morning when their sap level (and flavor) is highest. Thoroughly wash and dry the herbs—using a salad spinner works well. Then gather them in small bunches and tie them together. Put the herb bunches in a brown paper bag, poke small holes in the bag with a pencil point, and seal the bag to protect the herbs from dust, bugs, and sunlight. Hang the bags upside down in a warm and dry place, leaving enough room for the air to circulate. Then leave them alone for one to two weeks until the herbs are dry and brittle. Once they're dried, detach the leaves from the stems and chop finely with a knife or food processor. Transfer them to small jars with tight-fitting lids and store them in a cool, dark cupboard.

> To save time, you also can dry your herbs in a microwave, but they won't be quite as flavorful. Place a single layer of herbs on two sheets of white paper towel, without crowding them. Cover with a paper towel and microwave on high for 1 to 3 minutes. Check every 15 seconds to make sure they're not getting too dry or, even worse, igniting!

99. Buy seeds instead of seedlings.

Avid gardeners can easily spend hundreds of dollars every year buying new plants. You can buy a bag of geranium seeds for $1 and get twenty-five plants instead of paying $1.50 for individual plants. If twenty-five geraniums are too many (how could there ever be too many geraniums?), split the packet with a friend for even more cost savings.

100. Another freebie.

Join the Seed Savers Club sponsored by *Organic Gardening* magazine. This is an absolutely free service and a great way to obtain rare varieties and start correspondence with other gardening enthusiasts! If you have seeds of the type requested that you'd like to share, send five to twenty seeds to the names listed. In return, the sharers will send you the seeds they are offering. If you don't have anything to swap but would like to get some seeds, send a small, self-addressed padded envelope with adequate postage to receive seeds from someone else willing to share. Send your name, address, and the varieties you're offering or seeking to Seed Savers/Seed Sharers, *Organic Gardening Magazine,* 33 E. Minor Street, Emmaus, PA 18098.

101. Who needs this?

Don't spend money every year on useless annuals. Grow only perennials or self-sowing annuals that will replenish themselves. Your garden will grow fuller and more colorful each summer as these plants spread.

Here are ten hardy, self-seeding perennials that are perfect for frugal gardeners: alyssum, carnations, creeping phlox, daylilies, hollyhocks, hostas, orange glory flowers, shasta daisies, sweet william, and veronica. And for a great self-sowing annual you can't beat sweet peas—they're stunning climbers and have a long blooming season too.

102. Another freebie.

To celebrate Earth Day, the League of Women Voters has been handing out a wonderful "natural pesticide"—ladybugs! Ladybugs eat small insects as well as eggs and insect larvae, and will save you money by allowing you to use fewer chemical pest controls in your garden. The league recommends storing a jar full of ladybugs in the refrigerator (!) until you're ready to place them in the garden. Water your garden well and release the ladybugs at dusk. You can sprinkle them on tomatoes and other vegetables or plants that might be infested by bugs. Martha's daughter was captivated by the ladybugs and was thrilled to help them find homes in the garden. To find out if the league is distributing these bugs in your area, check your phone book to see if there's a local league chapter and give it a call. If not, ask your local garden shop if it sells ladybugs.

103. Save cash on your trash.

Make sure you recycle everything you can, now that many communities are charging extra for each garbage can you put out. And start a compost heap in an unused corner of your yard. Some states have started charging to haul away garden waste as well as household trash. At a fee of $1 to $2 per garbage bag, disposal charges can add up quickly every time you rake your leaves or trim your hedges.

If you don't have room for a compost heap, you can simply *double mow* over your grass clippings and then leave them on your lawn. The clippings are kind to your lawn—and to your wallet, since you won't have to buy any additional chemical fertilizers.

104. Give each of your children his or her own small garden plot.

There are many hidden benefits, if your backyard has a little room to spare. Not only will your kids have an absorbing outdoor project and get an early botany lesson, they're also much more likely to eat their vegetables if they've nurtured them themselves!

Kids love eating healthful snacks when they've grown them themselves. One of our friends planted plenty of raspberries, strawberries, green beans, and sweet cherry tomatoes, and her two daughters can't get enough of them. This sure beats buying pork rinds or other unhealthful snacks at $1.79 a bag.

105. Another freebie.

Make your own in-ground waterer and avoid the cost of a soaker hose. Take a coffee can or plastic milk jug and poke a hole in the bottom with a nail. Then bury the can up to the rim in the ground near your plant. (In the vegetable garden, you might want to sink a whole line of these cans between rows.) Instead of watering every day, simply fill the cans once or twice a week for slow, deep, in-ground watering. This trick also works for houseplants if you use a smaller can; it's especially useful if you go away for a week and don't want to come home to dead foliage.

106. Insulate with ivy.

Cut your heating and cooling costs by up to 30 percent, without adding insulation or weatherstripping. Proper use of fences, bushes, trees, and earth berms all can contribute to lower energy costs by manipulating sunlight, wind, and heat radiation. And if you have to spend money to improve energy efficiency, you might as well get double duty for your bucks with something that also looks attractive. To find out how to do it, call the Conservation and Renewable Energy Inquiry and Referral Service (1-800-523-2929) and request the free brochure "Landscaping for Energy Efficient Homes."

107. Divide the spoils.

Perennials like daylilies and irises that you can divide are a real boon to frugal gardeners because they propagate so easily. And unlike self-sowing seeds, the divided crowns stay right where you put them! Dividing them is simple enough: In the fall after all flowering is done, lift the crown clump out of the soil and separate it with a sharp garden spade. Voilà! Two for the price of one. Replant both halves and mulch well.

108. Another freebie.

Recycle plastic loops from soda or beer six-packs—hey, even frugal fanatics have a party every now and then—into a trellis. Tie the loops together end to end and side to side to make a climbing support for peas, beans, cucumbers, or even flowering vines. A trellis usually costs $20 for a six-foot section, so you'll be saving money at the same time you're keeping plastic out of the landfill.

109. Never buy fertilizer again.

If you or a friend have a fireplace or wood-burning store, just use the ashes instead of fertilizer in your garden. They are very high in potassium (also known as potash), which keeps plants vigorous and helps them resist a wide variety of diseases.

In the Nursery

Caring for Kids on a Tight Budget

110. Trade your time.

Find two or three other parents whose children seem reasonably polite and healthy and form a baby-sitting co-op. With movie tickets going for $7 and teenage sitters (if you can find one on a weekend night) costing $4 or more an hour, a simple evening out can easily run $40 to $50, especially if you are thinking of anything as radical as dinner too. By trading baby-sitting hours with another couple, you can cut the cost of a date with your spouse by one-third to one-half.

Or, instead of joining a formal co-op, you can just trade baby-sitting with a friend or neighbor. This works particularly well for at-home parents during the day, since teenage sitters are all in school. By trading sitting one or two mornings a week with a friend, you can get the chance to take a class, work part time, or just get some well-deserved time off, all without spending any money on baby-sitting.

111. Share a sitter.

If you are going out with another couple, gather all the children in one house (preferably already pajama'ed and with sleeping bags) and split the cost of the sitter, assuming of course that there will be a slight additional cost per hour for the extra children.

112. Use it twice for half the price.

Make an inexpensive bowling pin set for the kids, using two-liter plastic soda bottles filled with sand or pebbles. The advantage of this kind of bowling pin is that you can make the game easier or harder by adjusting how much weight you have in the bottle. Use a very small amount of sand and even the tiniest tot can bowl with a regular beach ball. You'll feel even better about your handiwork when you notice toy bowling sets selling for $25 at the toy store.

113. Another freebie.

Don't spring for expensive sets of cardboard blocks. We've seen these painted cardboard "bricks" advertised for as much as $40 (for forty-eight bricks). Yes, kids love to use blocks and boxes to build forts, castles, and so on. But why pay nearly $1 per block when you probably have all the boxes you need right in your basement or garage? Your own boxes also will come in an interesting variety of shapes and sizes, unlike the store-bought variety. Double your children's fun by encouraging them to decorate the boxes themselves with stickers, paint, and markers.

114. Make your own craft clay.

Happy kids require a lot of messy toys—the stickier the better. But that doesn't mean you have to bust your budget on all sorts of expensive store-bought arts and crafts materials (we recently saw a clay-and-ornaments kit selling for over $10). Make clay at home with cornstarch and baking soda (see recipe below). You can make several bowls and knead in food coloring to color the clay. Store the clay wrapped in a damp cloth in an airtight tub or airtight plastic bag in the refrigerator. Allow it to come to room temperature and knead it slightly before using again. This clay is not meant to be fired in a kiln. You can use it to build sculptures and bowls and even roll it out on waxed paper and cut it into ornamental shapes with a cookie cutter. You can stick beads and other decorations on it (use a little glue just to be sure they'll stick), and paint it when dry. *Warning:* This clay is not for eating, so don't give it to young kids.

HOMEMADE MODELING CLAY

1 cup cornstarch (or salt)

4 cups baking soda

1½ cups warm water

Combine the ingredients in a saucepan and stir until fairly smooth. Bring to a boil and simmer 1 minute while continuing to stir.

Pour the mixture into a pan or shallow bowl and cover with a damp cloth or paper towel to cool. It's ready to use once it's cool.

You can have fun making homemade Christmas tree ornaments by cutting craft clay with holiday cookie cutters, cutting out a small hole near the top while the clay is damp, and then letting it dry. When it is dry, help your kids paint the ornaments and tie colorful ribbon through the holes. Now you have a creative, useful, one-of-a-kind gift for your family or friends.

115. Make your own modeling dough at home.

It will cost you only pennies instead of $3 to $4 per jar. Use the recipe on page 58. Store your homemade dough in plastic yogurt containers with lids or Ziploc bags. It keeps longer in the refrigerator. Additional bonus: This craft recipe is not only cheap but safe—it's edible if you have an omnivorous toddler in the house.

HOMEMADE MODELING DOUGH

1 cup flour

½ cup salt

2 teaspoons cream of tartar

1 cup water

1–2 tablespoons vegetable oil

Several drops food coloring

Cook together all the ingredients except the vegetable oil in a small saucepan over medium heat for a few minutes until the dough bubbles. Cool slightly.

Knead in the vegetable oil by the teaspoonful until the dough is pliable. Add the food coloring. To make the neon colors kids love, increase the amount of food coloring.

116. Make your own craft paste.

Mix 1 cup white flour with 1 cup cold water in a saucepan. Simmer it over low heat until it is thick and creamy. Let it cool slightly and then use it right away for paper crafts or building papier-mâché sculptures with old newspaper strips. This paste can be stored in a covered plastic container in the refrigerator.

If you're feeling creative and thrifty and want to save $20, craft paste is perfect for making papier-mâché piñatas for your children's birthday parties.

117. Try making your kids' toys yourself.

Simple, imaginative patterns are available at reasonable prices from Toys and Joys (206-354-3448). There are patterns for a wide range of vehicles, from trucks to trains plus historical replicas, such as the Model T. In browsing through some children's catalogs, we discovered some pretty astronomical prices for wooden toys, including $92 for 62 unpainted hardwood blocks (!), $110 for a rocking horse, $250 for a set of "castle blocks," and $136.50 for a wooden dollhouse (without furniture). If these prices don't motivate you to get started, we don't know what will.

118. Forget paper towels for kid clean-up.

Use sponges and washcloths instead. At mealtimes (when all of us with young children to feed tend to need handy instant clean-up devices), keep a couple of washcloths around to wash sticky faces and hands instead of using throw-away paper towels. Depending on how adept (or should we be kind and say enthusiastic?) your little eaters are, you may be going through two or three rolls a week. At 70 cents a roll, that's $8 to $10 dollars of your monthly food budget that could be allocated toward more important things, like a night out at the movies. Not to mention that sponges and cloths are soft and kinder to babies' skin than harsh paper.

119. Trade toys.

Somehow, most children believe that their friends' toys are infinitely preferable to their own. A little judicious swapping can work wonders when bored kids complain "There's nothing to do." Or find out if your community has a toy lending library. These allow you to check out several toys for a few weeks at a nominal fee (many let you check them out for free!). Send a self-addressed stamped envelope to USA Toy Library Association, 2530 Crawford Avenue, Suite 111, Evanston, IL 60201, for a nationwide list of toy libraries.

120. Blow up a baby bed.

Portable baby cribs are popular, convenient, and often expensive—we've seen them advertised for as much as $110. If your child isn't crawling yet, here's a cheaper alternative: Use an inflatable pool ring lined with receiving blankets for your baby's traveling bed. This makes a soft, safe, and comfortable sleeping spot (as long as the room isn't drafty and you relegate any curious pets to another room). We just came across a $37.75 "sleep mat with rounded bumpers" that looks very similar to our "pool sleeper." Our version has the added advantage of packing down very small and light once deflated. You can use this for several months while you check the resale shops for a secondhand portable crib in good condition. This tip will save you between $31.75 and $106.00, depending on which kind of portable crib you decide *not* to buy.

121. Change your changing table.

When your last child is *finally* potty-trained, recycle that wooden changing table to store picture books, stuffed animals, puzzles, games, and so on. Paint the table in bold primary colors to help disguise its origins and to jazz up your child's room. This will save you $50 to $100, since you won't need to buy a bookcase or large toy box for all of the toys.

122. Who needs this?

Baby food reality check: A single serving of pureed carrots costs 45 cents a jar in our local supermarket. But for 39 cents, you can buy a bag of carrots and invest ten minutes in the following procedure to provide an entire week's worth of servings: Chop the raw carrots and microwave them in a covered dish with a small amount of water for five minutes. Then puree the cooked carrots in a blender or simply mash them thoroughly with a fork. Pour or scrape the pureed carrots into an ice cube tray and freeze. To make a single serving, simply pop out a "carrot cube," thaw in a heated dish or microwave, and voilà! baby food. This technique works equally well for other vegetables and even meat and vegetable mixes.

The approximate savings per week for homemade baby carrots is $2.50. The savings per year equal $140 just for this one meal item. If you do the same for Junior's other feedings, the savings can easily add up to over $500 a year.

123. Use it twice for half the price.

Instead of buying expensive portfolios in the school supply store to archive your children's artwork, simply use the cardboard tubes left over from wrapping paper. These tubes provide safe and sturdy storage. (Don't forget to date their drawings for posterity.) You'll save $12 to $15 by bypassing the cardboard portfolios.

124. Get a grip on broken glassware.

If you're tired of paying to replace glasses that your children drop and break, try this simple trick. (It's especially useful if you and your young kids are visiting Grandma or a friend who doesn't have a supply of sipper cups.) Help your children learn to hold the glasses by wrapping a simple rubber band or two around the glass. This really helps little hands get a secure grip. (Depending on what sort of entertaining you do, especially during playoff seasons, you might want to institute this feature for adults too.)

125. Shop garage sales for good-quality used sports equipment.

Your children usually will outgrow the equipment or get tired of the sport long before it's worn out. We prowled around our local sporting goods supply store recently and were surprised at some of the prices they were asking, including $35 for an official NBA basketball, $130 for a name-brand tennis racket, $20 for an aluminum bat, $35 for a baseball mitt, and $22 for a soccer ball. You can find most of these items at under $10 by keeping an eye out for neighborhood yard sales.

126. Give the gift of sanity.

Instead of buying expensive baby layettes for new parents, consider giving the priceless gift of sanity. Surprise close friends and family with a few coupons entitling them to your free babysitting services, which, depending on where you live, will be worth anything from $2 to $8 an hour. Chances are this gift will be their favorite!

127. Who needs this?

We've seen ads in parenting magazines for a spray bottle of "monster spray." Designed to scare monsters away from a child's room, the bottle bears a scary drawing of a monster's face. The spray, however, consists only of water and a little bubblegum scent. It's a creative solution to helping a child get rid of nighttime fears—but for $6.95 a bottle, we'll use our own spray bottle and a little imagination, thank you.

Managing and Maintaining Your Biggest Investment

128. Want to sell your house?

Don't get caught in the trap of throwing money at it in an attempt to make it more salable. New family rooms and master baths, which usually run overtime and overbudget, are projects you should do when you move into that fixer-upper, so you can enjoy them yourselves. According to *Metropolitan Home,* the cheapest cosmetic improvements—fresh paint, new carpets, and a few attractive plants out front—have the greatest payback (sometimes as much as 1,000 percent) because they make a good impression on prospective buyers and present your house as well cared for.

There's an added incentive to making cosmetic improvements just before selling: Ordinarily, these improvements are merely considered maintenance and cannot be deducted from your costs in the house for tax purposes. However, all improvements, including paint and plantings, made within ninety days of selling can be deducted from the selling price when you compute your capital gain on the transaction.

129. Stopped-up sink?

Don't call the plumber—yet. You may be able to remove the obstruction yourself with two simple techniques. First, try plunging the sink. Make sure there's a good five inches of water in the sink (run more in if there's not) and then place your bathroom plunger over the drain and compress it. Lift up no more than one inch and press again. Keep the cup in the water at all times. If you have a double sink, block the other drain with a wet rag so you don't lose pressure. Try plunging for at least five minutes—it may take that long to rock or suck the obstruction free. If plunging doesn't work, try cleaning out the trap. The trap is the U-shape section of pipe directly under your sink. Some traps have a simple clean-out plug right in the bottom; others have two ring nuts that you must loosen to remove the entire trap. Either way, the operation takes no more than five minutes. Remember to have a big pan under the trap to catch the water that will come out. Chances are good that you will find your obstruction in the trap. Buying and using a $5 plunger instead of calling a plumber can save you between $50 and $70 for each clog.

130. Advanced plumbing: The snake trick.

Use a plumber's "snake" or "closet auger" to rout out your plumbing lines, either because they are obstructed far down the line or as a twice-yearly maintenance procedure to prevent problems. A snake is a flexible cable with a hook on one end and a turning handle on the other. It is usually used on sinks (with the trap open). When the handle is turned the snake turns, and you push it into the pipe while turning. Usually the obstruction is punched through, but sometimes you actually can grab it with the hook. A closet auger is similar to a snake but is even more flexible so you can use it on toilets. A snake or auger sells for around $15; a plumber's visit can cost five times as much.

131. Easy appliance repair.

Don't take appliances with broken plugs into the local repair shop to be fixed—do it yourself. Plugs can be repaired easily with replacement units sold in hardware stores. (Snap-on plugs sell for as little as $1.09 apiece.) You don't need to strip wire or split ends. You just cut the ends of the wire square with a knife or scissors (we use kitchen shears), and feed the ends through the housing of the replacement unit and into a ready-made opening in the points. Then you shove the points back into the housing, and it's done. You'll save $15 to $25 by avoiding the repair shop.

132. Who needs this?

Yet another pilgrimage to the local hardware store (in search of the one size screw nobody has in stock) turned up a nifty new item on the shelves: a flexible, one-inch-diameter plastic tube promoted as the ideal item to organize a clutter of appliance cords. Cost: $14.95. No thanks. We'll just keep using the cardboard sleeves left over from toilet paper and paper towel rolls.

133. Smart buys save money.

This item may be worth the price—a sound-activated light control called the Sonar Socket. It can be used to turn on a light by clapping your hands, but aside from this party trick, it's more valuable use is to ward off intruders. The unit can be adjusted to respond to sounds from quiet tapping to breaking glass. The light will go on immediately for three minutes, then reset. Used in conjunction with a light timer, the Sonar Socket at $22 may help prevent big losses from theft.

134. Make it last longer.

More hoses and electrical cords fail every year from improper use and storage than from any other reason. Extend the life of your hoses and extension cords by coiling them the right way. Let

An inferior-quality ⅝″ 50-foot vinyl garden hose costs around $15; a good-quality all-weather rubber version costs $32. At these prices, it makes sense to double the life of your hose simply by coiling it properly.

the coil fall as it wants, instead of twisting it into figure eights or around your forearm.

135. Cheap decorating 101.

Sure, the days when you considered a Jimi Hendrix poster the ultimate decoration for the living room are probably long gone, but beautiful posters are still one of the best ways to get a big bang for your decorating buck, especially for children's rooms, the den, or a home office. One mail order source, United Communications, provides extremely handsome posters that are educational too, such as a dinosaur poster of more than twenty species with accompanying text, hummingbirds, fish, cats, dogs, roses, annual flowers—you get the picture. A selection of prints from the British Museum is also available. United frames the prints for an additional charge, but you can probably do that yourself cheaper at home. To request a catalog, contact United at 644 Merrick Road, Lynbrook, NY 11563 (1-800-433-7523).

Bubble wraps are not only good for packing breakables, they also provide wonderful tic-tac-toe boards for car or train trips, especially for young children who can't be trusted around upholstery with sharp pencils or markers. Take a few moments to outline some grids on the wrap with an indelible marker, show the kids how to pop a bubble with their fingers, and they're off!

136. Use it twice for half the price.

Be an educated packrat. Don't hoard everything, only things that you really can reuse. For instance, while huge stacks of cardboard boxes do have an undeniable allure, not all boxes should be saved. Some, such as gift boxes and sturdy shipping boxes, are worth the effort because between Christmas, Chanukah, and birthdays, plenty of opportunities to reuse them will occur.

Our local Mail Boxes store charges between $5 to $7 apiece for medium and large boxes. If you ship twenty gifts for birthdays and holidays during an average year, you'll save at least $100 by reusing the boxes you already have.

137. Always get at least three bids for service work.

You may be astounded at the variation in charges for such standard items as pumping a septic tank, reflashing a chimney, or putting a set of braces on Little Fang's front teeth.

Don't be discouraged if your first forays into competitive bidding don't immediately result in substantial savings. For instance, while all three septic services in our area charge the same $125 to pump a tank, furnace maintenance is quite another story. Three calls for a fall furnace clean-up resulted in quotes of $59, $50, and finally $42. Using the cheapest services is like getting every fourth cleaning free. Keep calling—you too will luck out eventually.

138. Reduce your rent.

If you live in an apartment, get your rent reduced in return for doing small maintenance chores, such as trimming the bushes, shoveling the walk in winter, or putting out the trash.

139. Reverse yourself.

Look into getting a "reverse mortgage" if you are over sixty-two years old and still own the big house from your child-rearing days, but taxes and other housing costs are getting increasingly difficult to pay. With this type of mortgage, the lender pays you a set amount of money every month for a certain number of years, based on the value of your home. And you won't have to repay the bank until you sell your house or move. The major drawback, of course, is that you'll no longer be able to pass the house along to your children or grandchildren—but it may be worth it if it enables you to stay in your home instead of being forced to sell it because of rising costs. For more information on reverse mortgages and a list of more than 150 lenders across the country that specialize in them, send $1 and a self-addressed stamped envelope to: The National Center for Home Equity Conversion, 7373 147th Street West, Suite 115, Apple Valley, MN 55124.

If you tie your reverse mortgage into an annuity program for yourself, you also can ensure that the bank will continue to pay you monthly if you go into a nursing home.

140. Want to get rid of that water in your basement?

Nine times out of ten the culprit is poor grading and overflowing gutters rather than groundwater seepage. Before you call the concrete pumper, carefully check all gutters and your downspout to make sure they aren't clogged and are directing water away from the house. The ground at the foundation should slope away from the house and be clear of plantings. You can save $200 to $300 by cleaning out your gutters and doing a little scraping with a hoe instead of calling the basement waterproofers. If you still have water after correcting all these other problems, then you may indeed need the waterproofers.

141. Don't replace your screens—patch 'em.

Bothered by pesky bugs that have found their way through your screen doors or windows? We've found a cheap way to fix that without replacing the entire screens. You can buy a set of twenty-five hook-on screen patches for only $5 from the Vermont Country Store catalog (1-802-362-2400). A new screen door costs between $60 and $100 (plus around $75 for installation), so you can save as much as $170 by patching those holes yourself.

142. Get double duty for your dollars.

Use toothpaste to get rid of your young artists' crayon drawings on your painted walls. The gentle abrasives in toothpaste really work, but if you have wallpaper you might want to test a small spot first. Toothpaste also is effective in getting rid of the rings on your good dining room table caused by wet glassware.

> Even better, invest in washable Crayola markers, paint, and crayons in the first place, so you don't have to expend much time or energy cleaning the walls, your kids' clothes, and your lace tablecloths. Crayola art supplies may cost a dollar or two more than the cheap drugstore versions, but they're well worth it.

143. Resurrect the old-fashioned rag bag.

Keep a rag bag of old clothes that are too ratty to resell or give away to use for cleaning, polishing, painting dropcloths, and the like. Old kitchen towels and underwear make great rags. Your kids can also use your old worn shirts as painting smocks, which will save you big bucks in laundry and replacement costs for their good clothes.

144. Reach for the bleach.

Bleach has many more uses than just getting your clothes clean. Try using a small amount of laundry bleach diluted with water instead of pricey "general-purpose cleaners." You can make a highly effective cleaning agent by adding 1½ ounces of bleach to 1 gallon of water. Bleach and water work just as well as store-bought cleaners. (Many of the name brands use bleach as an active ingredient, in fact.) If you use the specified concentration of bleach in water, one gallon of bleach will last for forty-two cleaning sessions. But do make sure that kids and pets stay away from the mixture; like other cleaners, it's highly poisonous.

145. Make it last longer.

Don't throw out that mildewed and scaley shower curtain yet. Though these curtains can be notoriously difficult to clean, here's a technique that has a pretty good success rate and can save you the $20 you'd have to spend on a new shower curtain (not to mention the $50 you'll end up spending on new towels to match that new curtain). Remove the rings from the curtain and throw it into your washing machine with ½ cup detergent, ½ cup white vinegar, and 2 rough towels. Wash on the regular cycle but hang to dry. The vinegar provides the chemical muscle, and often the towels provide just the additional scrubbing action you need. Do this every few months, to keep your curtain relatively free of mildew and soap scum.

When the shower curtain is finally beyond use in the bathroom, you can still press it into service as a splatter guard under a high chair or as a dropcloth for small painting projects.

146. Make your own fabric softener sheets.

Clothes tossed with sheets do seem softer and smell better, but you pay dearly for the convenience. In just a few minutes you can make your own by pouring three capfuls of cheap generic liquid softener into a bowl of water. Stir until well mixed and then dunk several washcloths into the solution. Ring the washcloths out and throw them directly into the dryer, or make a batch and allow them to dry for future use. A large bottle of liquid softener (selling for around $2.40) will last at least three times longer than a box of forty fabric softener sheets that cost the same amount.

147. Use it twice for half the price.

If you must use store-bought fabric softener sheets, reuse them at least twice. Then save these used sheets from several dryings and use them all in one big load for a third and final time. That way you know you're really getting your money's worth out of them. Depending on how many loads you do a week, you could save from $20 to $60 a year.

148. Another freebie.

Want to avoid spending anything on cleaners for the mirrors and windows in your bathroom? Easy. Simply get in the habit of wiping down those surfaces with your damp towel after your shower or bath. The residual steam in the room will make cleaning a snap. Get every member of your household into this habit too—that way you'll save money and your own time and energy.

149. D.I.Y. (Do it yourself).

Here's a tip from a reputable Oriental rug cleaner: Instead of sending out your rugs for dry cleaning if a pet (or small child) leaves a urine stain on the rug, buy a big bottle of 3 percent hydrogen peroxide at your grocery or drugstore. First apply water to the stain. If that doesn't work, then blot the peroxide on the stain (do not dilute with water) and let it dry. Don't scrub vigorously—just apply the peroxide gently with a sponge or rag. It may take several applications, but the stain will lighten nicely. The quicker you treat the stain, the more effective this treatment will be.

150. Smart buys save money.

Baking soda is the best single household buy you can make. It can get rid of coffee and tea stains in cups; help activate bleach to get your clothes really clean; clean stained kitchen counters, cutting boards, and microwave oven interiors; polish silver; put out a grease fire or douse your barbecue; clean the insides of ice buckets and coolers; help remove burned food from pans; and absorb food or cigarette smoke odors. Baking soda on a damp cloth will clean your car's windows and headlights—and even take away "that smell" when added to a pet's bathwater. At $1 a box it costs less than a quarter of what commercial scrubs and polishes cost.

151. Make your own ceramic tile cleansing paste for pennies.

Mix ⅔ baking soda to ⅓ bleach, and save $2.50 over the cost of commercial tile cleaner.

152. Consider your rug rats when buying carpeting.

If you have kids or dogs, never, ever, ever even think about buying white carpeting, couches, or bedspreads. We also strongly disagree with people who tell you to buy "neutral" beige or light gray rugs—both show stains like crazy. Martha used to have carpeting called "English pewter" (a lovely blue-gray color) that hid muddy footprints and food spills much more effectively. Or consider getting a carpet with a small repeating pattern, which also masks stains nicely. Our local carpet cleaning firm charges 22

Avoid all-wool rugs like the plague—they cost much more than blended polyester/nylon rugs and are nearly impossible to clean. In fact, some carpet cleaners refuse to tackle them at all. Finally, take a tip from car dealers and spray your fabric sofa and chairs with Scotchgard spray before letting your kids or pets anywhere near them.

cents a square foot. If you have 500 square feet of carpeting, you'll shell out $110 every time it needs a steam cleaning. Buying a darker, stain-resistant carpet to begin with can cut the number of times you'll need to call the cleaning service in half.

153. Smart buys save money.

Vinegar and water can remove perspiration stains from clothes (spray just before putting in the wash); clean surfaces and glass doors of ovens and other appliances (including your TV screen); unclog a steam iron; remove dirt on upholstered furniture; clean out your coffeemaker and tea kettle; remove sticky labels from glassware; and clean bathroom tiles. Besides being versatile, vinegar is cheap: 99 cents for a bottle versus $3.49 for wash stain remover or $2.79 for window washing solution.

Never buy commercial brands of window washing solution again. Make your own from this simple, old-time recipe: ½ cup white vinegar or ammonia to 1 gallon water.

154. Renovation is not just for houses.

If a favorite household item starts falling apart, see if you can replace part of it instead of buying a new one. For example, Martha and her husband have a ten-year-old feather and down comforter that has been leaking feathers for a year or two and is getting pretty thin in places. They really need it to stay warm during those bitter Chicago winters. Rather than buy a new down comforter for $200 to $300, they called a couple of bedding catalogs specializing in down and found they could buy a pound of replacement feathers for $10. That's enough feathers to keep them toasty for years to come.

Here's another example: You can rescue an old popcorn maker that has developed large cracks in its plastic dome top. Order a new top for around $5 from the manufacturer instead of buying a brand-new machine for $19.95.

155. Smart buys save money.

On the other hand, avoid spending money repairing old electronic equipment. Investing in a new, improved TV, VCR, or stereo is often more cost-effective in the long run. Say you bought a two-head VCR eight years ago for $350, and it's starting to mangle your videotapes. You can get much more for your money by buying a new VCR instead of sinking your money into an aging piece of equipment. Since the technology has improved greatly over the years, you could get a four-head, stereo VCR for $50 less than you paid for your first VCR.

156. Battle bugs with borax.

Instead of calling in an exterminator, try a simple, old-fashioned remedy when you're beset with beetles: borax. In concentrated form, borax kills roaches, silverfish, ants, and other crawling bugs, and it doesn't have that strong, sickly sweet odor you get from other insecticides. Just sprinkle it near your doorways, on windowsills, behind appliances in the kitchen, near cracks in the skirting board, and other places where bugs tend to congregate. They'll take the powder with them back to their nests, where it can kill the whole colony.

Borax is effective for months and is not toxic to kids and pets if you follow the directions. You can find it in the Vermont Country Store catalog at 802-362-2400. When we called Orkin exterminators, we were given a quote of $140 for an initial treatment, plus $38 every month for a follow-up treatment! That's an annual cost of $596. Or you can buy your own borax for $4.25 a pound.

Saving Energy Equals Saving Money

157. Don't get sold on solar energy.

Unless you are building from scratch, retrofitting a house for active solar may be so costly that you never recoup your investment. Solar panel and converter systems can cost thousands of dollars. For retrofitters, going solar makes good sense in only a few applications—tile floors in the sunroom, solar lights at the foot of a long driveway where the cost of running gas or electric lines would be prohibitive, an easily installed Copper Cricket roof-mount water heater, and solar-activated attic and roof fans are usually good places to start without emptying your wallet.

158. Install a heat window on your dryer venting hose.

This will help capture heat and much-needed humidity for your house during the dry winter months.

> Use silver duct tape to attach an old panty hose leg over your washer hose and dryer vent to catch lint and hair before it gets into your plumbing and your air.

159. Gear the house down when you're out of town.

Turn down the heat or air conditioning, turn off the water heater (as much as 20 percent of your utility bill can be for the water heater alone, so a few days "off the grid" really can make a difference), and pull the plug on appliances with clocks that use electricity. When you're away for several weeks, you also might want to shut off water to appliances in case a hose bursts while you're gone. And turn down the ringer on your phones to hide the telltale sound of a frequently ringing phone. But remember to leave one or two lights on a timer and the radio playing softly on an all-talk station. No matter how much you save on utilities, it won't be worth it if your house looks so unoccupied that it gets robbed while you're away.

Here's another easy burglar-foiling tip that most people don't think of. Locking your doors may not be enough if your windows are fairly easy to break into. You can lock wooden sash windows quickly by screwing the two halves of the window together with a large screw. This will make it impossible to lift the window from the outside. Simply remove the screws when you return home.

160. Smart buys save money.

If you are unfortunate enough to live in an area with hard water, invest in a water softener. It will save you money in the end because your pipes and clothes will last longer and you won't have to pay out big bucks to plumbers, dry cleaners, and beauty salons for expensive hair treatments to counter the corrosive effects of the hard water.

161. Who needs this?

Don't ever buy the expensive "rust-out" brine blocks for your water softener. For under $5, you can purchase a big tub of plumbers' rust remover powder at a hardware store that you mix up with water and throw in the softener yourself.

162. Smart buys save money.

Everyone knows that south-facing windows can help your house gain solar heat during the winter, but you may not realize that all of that gain will be lost overnight if you don't also install insulating drapes or shades. So, enjoy your winter sun during the day, but come nightfall, pull those drapes! (Martha's family chose elegant velvet curtains with a hidden but practical thermal lining for their living and dining room.)

163. Get more light for less wattage.

If you have a light in the house that's nearly always on—perhaps in the living room or kitchen—invest in a compact fluorescent bulb instead of a standard light bulb. Compact fluorescents can be screwed right into ordinary light fixtures and can last for years. Although they cost more initially, compact fluorescents are much cheaper to operate and much longer-lasting than incandescent bulbs.

The average incandescent bulb (75 watts) lasts for around 750 hours; an 18-watt compact fluorescent bulb, while initially more expensive to purchase, gives the same amount of light, uses less energy, and lasts for around 10,000 hours! Depending on energy costs in your area, that translates into $30 to $50 savings on each bulb over the course of its life.

164. Always air-dry.

If you must use a dishwasher, make sure you let the dishes air-dry instead of using the heat-dry option. Most dishwasher models allow you to make that choice.

Economically, it just doesn't make sense to run the dishwasher without a full load, so if you're looking for something to fill out a rack, put your cutting boards in. Not only will they be clean, but they'll be sterilized too, which is very important if you use them for cutting chicken and other meat.

165. Time your appliance usage.

Some utility companies charge less for electricity during certain off-peak hours. Call your local gas and electric utilities to find out if they offer discounts and what those hours are; then try to run greedy appliances (computers, water heaters, dishwashers, clothes dryers, etc.) during those times.

166. Be bold with the cold.

Water, that is. Water heating costs make up about 30 percent (more if your water heater is electric!) of the cost of doing laundry, so take an extra minute to sort your laundry into cold water/hot water washes, not just light and dark loads. If just half of your loads can be washed in cold water, you will be able to cut your cleaning costs by 15 percent. In addition, cold water is kinder to your clothes, so this washing method will help them last longer.

Even if your utility doesn't offer discounts, you can make the most of your energy consumption by timing your usage. For instance, you can line-dry clothes in the summer and use your dryer only in the winter, when your direct vent kit actually can add welcome humidity and heat to cold, stale indoor air. And bread baking in the oven on a cold winter evening makes the kitchen a cozy place to congregate, allowing you to turn the thermostat down in other areas of the house.

Always set your rinse cycle for cold water—warm rinse water doesn't get clothes any cleaner. Presoaking works much better on heavily soiled loads.

167. Smart buys save money.

If you are buying a new dryer, one worthwhile option is a moisture sensor that automatically shuts the appliance off when clothes are dry. Dryers are real gas-guzzlers, so your goal should be to run them as efficiently as possible.

You can make efficiency improvements to your dryer even if it is an older model without a moisture sensor. Try to gang items of similar drying times together, so that you don't run any load longer than you have to. Simply separating out towels and denims, two items with notoriously long drying times, should allow you to run the rest of your loads for much shorter—and less costly—times.

168. Cool it.

Your fridge operates seven days a week, twenty-four hours a day, which makes it the second-hungriest appliance to run in your house (after the water heater). You can keep its appetite down by keeping the various zones in it at their proper temperatures (check your owner's manual), keeping the freezer full (fill out empty space with ice bags to help hold the cold), and vacuuming the coils behind the refrigerator every few months. Clean coils let your unit operate more efficiently, which means it will use less expensive energy.

Another way to save on cooling costs is to make sure that your refrigerator's door seal is airtight. You can test this by closing the door over a piece of paper (leave half sticking out of the door). If the paper can be pulled out easily, the latch or seal may need replacing.

169. Insulate your hot water pipes.

This reduces heat loss and keeps your expensive water heater from working so hard. Also, put an insulating blanket around your water heater to help keep your gas bill down. This works all year-round and is not just for people who live in subarctic climates.

Improve the efficiency of your water heater by getting out a hose and draining a bucket or two of water from it once or twice a year. Sediment from the heated water does tend to build up in the bottom of the tank, which makes the heater work harder and less efficiently.

170. Another freebie.

Everyone knows that it's cheaper to make calls at certain times of the day or night, but who can remember those times? Different carriers have different reduced rate times, which makes keeping track of costs especially difficult. Put a sticker or note with your telephone service's discount calling times on your phones as a reminder. Sometimes waiting just five minutes to make a call can add up to big savings.

Cut down on long-distance calls by using an egg timer to help keep you aware of how long you've been talking. Having your mate hovering over your shoulder giving you significant glances and making a wind-it-up hand gesture also can help you remember when it's time to hang up the phone.

171. Don't just moan about the phone bill.

Take three months' worth of long-distance phone bills and review them to see if the majority of your calls are being made to just one or two area codes. If so, check with your long-distance carrier to see if it has a discount program for frequently called numbers. If it doesn't, find another carrier that does.

172. Stop dialing your dollars away.

Don't pay for phone company services you don't really need. Phone companies now offer a stunning array of executive-type services for your home, such as Call Waiting, Call Forwarding, Three Way Dialing, and Caller ID. You probably could hire a personal assistant to answer and screen all your calls for what you are paying out for these special—and usually useless—services.

Don't let your teens talk you into Call Waiting as a means of ensuring that your emergency call will come through their nightly gabfests. In a true emergency an operator will always cut in, and meanwhile your kids are running up big bills.

173. Let others do the work—for free.

Having trouble figuring out which long-distance carrier has the best discount package for your calling patterns? Let the companies do it for you. Send them two or three previous bills and let each company come up with its best plan for you. For instance, the best carrier for Martha, who makes lots of international calls to in-laws in England, is different from the best one for Darcie, who does most of her long-distance dialing to just one area code in her ancestral New Jersey.

Here are the 800 numbers of some of the biggest long-distance phone companies. Send them a sample bill and ask for their rate card: AT&T: 1-800-222-0300; MCI: 1-800-333-4000; Sprint: 1-800-521-4949.

174. Stop wasting rain down the drain.

You can buy downspout inserts for around $12 that will help you channel wasted rainwater into your own barrel, bucket, or garbage can. This water can be saved for your garden, houseplants, or even for washing your car. It particularly makes sense if you're plagued by high water bills in your region of the country and blessed with a reasonable amount of rainfall. In the Chicago area, water bills run around $50 a month—or $600 a year—so we try to use the free water that falls from the sky whenever possible.

175. Tanks a lot.

If you have a tabletop gas grill for barbecuing, you can get a $12 adapter hose at a hardware store that lets you use large tanks of propane gas. These large tanks are refillable and much more economical than buying smaller tanks. You can buy a 20-pound propane tank at your hardware store for a one-time cost of $20. After that, whenever the propane runs out, you can get the tank refilled at most hardware stores for around $10. Standard-size 14.1-ounce propane cylinders cost around $3.60 for less than a pound; filling your own tank costs only 50 cents a pound. This large tank also lasts and lasts. Martha's family used to go through nine or ten small propane cylinders on their gas grill per summer, but they've used their large cylinder for three years without needing a refill.

176. Another D.I.Y.

Insulate your attic yourself. It's fairly easy to do and saves you a bundle, both in installation and heating costs. We were shocked to discover that an average roof is less than an inch thick. There's not much between your family and the outside elements. If you have three inches or less of old insulation, you'll need to add your own to keep the house warm and snug. When installing it, make sure you don't insulate on top of eave vents or lighting fixtures. Fit the insulation between the wooden studs, trim it at the bottom of the wall, and then staple to the edges of the stud. Don't forget to wear a dust mask to avoid breathing in the fiberglass.

This investment will pay for itself within a few years—and you'll cut your home heating costs by 5 to 30 percent, depending on how severe your winters are and how much insulation your house had before. (If you used to pay $100 a month on your winter heating bills, for example, installing insulation can save you $5 to $30 a month.) Another plus is that your furnace won't have to work so hard once your house is adequately insulated, so this project will also help prolong the life of your furnace.

177. Venting makes sense.

While you're up in the attic, add an automatic whole-house ventilating fan to cool the house—even if you have air conditioning. Attic ventilation can decrease the cost of cooling your home dramatically, since temperatures in an unventilated attic can reach over 140 degrees on a hot summer day! The fan will push this unwanted hot air back outside, where it belongs, and costs only about 30 cents a day to run. It costs at least three times that to operate an air conditioner, so any time your attic fan limits your need for AC, you're saving money. For example, our neighbors' AC used to be on all day during July and August. Since they installed an attic fan, their whole house stays cooler and the thermostat doesn't usually kick in until late afternoon. Their summer electric bills dropped by over one-third.

178. Vacuum your vents.

Keep all heating vents and filters—especially the return air filter—clean. The efficiency of your heating/cooling system can be reduced by as much as 25 percent by dirty, clogged filters—and that translates directly into more money spent on running the system.

179. Dodge the drafts.

Fine Homebuilding magazine estimates that air leaks and drafts can contribute to as much as 30 to 40 percent of the heat lost from the house. That means you're wasting a third of the money you spend on heating your home! So remember to caulk and seal and use glass or plastic storm windows in the winter.

A tube of caulk costs around $2.50, making caulking one of the most cost-effective ways you can weatherize your home. Since new cracks in your house can occur every year, caulking and adding weatherstripping are good fall projects to tackle before the cold weather sets in. According to the Department of Energy, adding caulking and weatherstripping can save you up to 10 percent on your annual energy costs. Not only will your house be more heat efficient, but a less drafty house can be comfortably kept five to ten degrees cooler, so you will get double duty for your insulation dollars.

180. Making small efforts to conserve water can really add up.

- Remember to shut the faucet off while you are brushing your teeth—you'll save gallons every week.
- Fill a 1-liter jug with water and put it in your toilet tank as a quick and easy way to cut down on water use each time you flush.
- Take daily showers instead of baths. Filling an average bath takes about 30 gallons of water. Installing and using a low-flow showerhead can reduce your water use to just 15 gallons per shower. You can save nearly 2,000 gallons of hot water a year by substituting one shower for one bath every day!

- Install an aerator in your kitchen sink faucet. It'll help you reduce your use of water in the kitchen by 50 percent, and you probably won't even notice the lower flow pressure.

About 15 percent of an average home's utility bill is spent on heating water. Cutting down on hot water use in the bath and kitchen will reduce the amount of money you spend on heating your water dramatically, so you save two ways.

181. Install mood lighting.

Add dimmer switches to your bedrooms and dining room. Not only is dim lighting more romantic, it's also satisfyingly frugal!

182. We're fans of house fans.

On those rare refreshingly cool summer nights, put a large fan in an upstairs or bedroom window and leave a downstairs window open. This will pull the cooler air into the house and leave it comfortable at a fraction of what it would cost to leave the air conditioner running all night.

183. Conserve your energy.

When buying a new appliance that can be expensive to run, such as a refrigerator, furnace, washing machine, or dishwasher, don't forget to check the yellow-and-black EnergyGuide label. Most of us have probably seen these tags but overlooked them in favor of the price tag. If you take the time to study this label, which legally must be posted, you'll learn approximately how much the appliance costs to run each year. By comparing these costs among different models, you may find a model that costs a bit more initially but is significantly cheaper to run over the long haul.

184. Ask yourself if you can downgrade.

We know a woman who never replaced her dishwasher when it broke. With two growing boys and lots of family entertaining to do, at one time she really needed it. But now that it's just her and her husband, it often takes a week to fill the damn thing. When it broke, she found she didn't miss it. And Martha's family recently found they didn't need their old water softener anymore when their community switched from hard well water to much softer water from Lake Michigan. You can make a similar test by trying to do without an appliance when it breaks (unless of course it's your furnace in the middle of a midwestern winter) and see if you really need it.

185. Buy a fridge with a freezer on top.

When you absolutely have to buy a new refrigerator, the model you choose can really have an impact on your home's utility costs. Top-freezer refrigerators are about 35 percent cheaper to run than side-by-side models, since the freezer capacity is generally smaller. If you keep the fridge away from the stove, dishwasher, and other heat-producing appliances, you can save even more energy because it won't have to work quite as hard to keep cool.

186. Is it possible to save money at home by building a home?

Not if you have to contract out for the work. But if you have carpentry skills and, like Tom Sawyer, have friends who can be talked into helping you "whitewash the fence," you can realize considerable savings by acquiring your home through a kit. The most interesting one we have seen comes from Timberline Geodesics (1-800-DOME-HOME) of Berkeley, California. It will sell you the hardware, struts, and plans for a 1,500-square-foot dome for $4,195. For $6,795, you can get a complete dome shell kit that includes all the lumber precut. This company claims that its structures can be assembled easily by two people without previous construction experience because it uses precast connecting hardware and precut, color-coded struts. As anyone who has spent time in domes knows, they have fabulous vaulted ceilings, great light, and good energy efficiency, though privacy and noise can be a problem. And since domes use a third less material to enclose a given space than a frame house, they're very thrifty. If you want a vacation home or lakeside hideaway but can't afford regular construction costs, a dome kit might be the way to go.

187. Be realistic about selling your own real estate.

Everyone will tell you that you can save big bucks by selling your home yourself and thereby avoiding the broker's 6 to 8 percent fee. What no one tells you is that it may take you twice as long, since you have to place the ads and do the showings yourself. In addition, prospective buyers shopping with a broker will never get shown your home, since brokers know they won't get a cut of your profits if the deal is made. If you have the time and energy to manage selling your home yourself, by all means do so. However, if you're under the gun for a quick sale, or if your schedule doesn't provide you with the time to do showings, consider listing with a discount real estate broker. By agreeing to do some of the work involved in selling your home, you can whittle down the agent's share of the proceeds.

The Chicago Tribune recently reported on Help-U-Sell, a discount brokerage with 400 franchises nationwide. It charges a set fee of around $3,000 (although that can vary in different branches), and you don't need to pay anything until closing time. This company will run newspaper ads, list your home in their

> **W***HY U.S.A.* is a franchised brokerage that for a fee of $990 assists sellers if the sellers find their own buyers. Since finding the buyer is the hardest part, we're not sure what these people can do for you in terms of contract negotiations or paperwork that your own lawyer couldn't do already for several hundred dollars less. In any case, make sure you read your contract with brokers carefully to be clear on just what they are doing for you, what it will cost, and whose interests they represent.

publications, and help you with negotiations with buyers. You may pay an additional fee if you opt to have your house included in the Multiple Listing Service. Check your phone book to see if any discount brokerages operate in your area.

188. Smart buys save money.

Go ahead, spend a little extra and buy a "set-back" thermostat for your house. Depending on the season, these thermostats automatically turn the heat down (or turn the air-conditioning setting up) when you're asleep and when you're out of the house during the day. Digital thermostats are particularly flexible—you can program separate temperatures for weekends and weekdays as well as for different times of day. The major benefits of set-back thermostats are that they can get the house nice and cozy for you before you wake up in the morning, and they reliably turn themselves down every time you tell them to. If you have a manual thermostat and are running late for your train in the morning, you probably won't remember to take the time to reset it—so trading up to an electronic model can save money in the long run.

189. Fetch your firewood for free.

Many of our national forests will issue you a permit that allows you to pick up downed and dead trees. The cost of the permit is nominal—just make sure you have it with you when you go to collect your wood. For more information on the deadwood program nearest you, contact the USDA Forest Service, Public Affairs Department, 14th Street and Independence Avenue SW, Box 96090, Washington, DC 20090.

190. Do your own energy audit.

You can spend $100 to have a commercial outfit come and check your house for air leaks, or you can spend 69 cents for a box of utility candles and check it out yourself. Pass a lighted candle slowly around door frames, outlets, and window sashes. If the flame dances about, that area is in need of caulking and weatherstripping. Mark the sites of air leaks with chalk or masking tape, so you can come back and fix them at your leisure.

191. Who needs this?

Small under-the-sink instant water heaters are a popular—but pricey—way to eliminate the waste of running the water until it gets hot. Instead of spending $225 to save $5, why don't you just get in the habit of using that first minute of not-yet-hot running water for a legitimate use? For instance, in the morning it's easy to brush your teeth from the hot water tap to get things running for your face wash or shave. In the evening, fill the teapot or water your indoor plants from the hot water tap before you do the dishes. Then your dishwater will be warm, and you won't have wasted any water getting it that way.

192. Don't pay the pilot.

Reduce your cooking gas costs by almost one-third with absolutely no effort on your part. When buying a gas range, choose a model that uses electric ignition instead of a pilot light. Running your stove's pilot light twenty-four hours a day, seven days a week can account for as much as 30 percent of your cooking gas usage.

193. Put a damper on chimney heat loss.

Forgetting to close your chimney damper after a fire can exhaust more air from your house than an open window. Not only will you lose all the good heat the fire gave you, but extra warmth will be drawn up—and out!—from every other room in the house. The trick is remembering to close the damper each time you have a fire. At a nearby fireplace accessories store, we came across a nifty little brass sign on a chain that you can hang next to your fireplace. On one side, it says "Damper open" and the other side says "Damper closed." This small sign can be just the reminder you need. If you can't find a brass sign or want a less expensive alternative, make your own out of cardboard and construction paper and hang it on a yarn string.

194. Goose down your thermostat.

Buy a really nice, thick goosedown comforter (available from discount linen stores and catalogs for around $100 to $200). Then get in the habit of turning down the heat at least 5 degrees (preferably 8 or 10 degrees) just before you go to bed. Since every 1 degree you drop your thermostat saves you 3 percent on your fuel bill, the comforter will pay for itself the very first winter. Your savings and snuggling enjoyment will continue for years and years.

195. Listen to your mother.

She told you to cover dishes in your fridge—and she was right. If you don't, moisture will be drawn from the foods and condense on the refrigerator's coils. This condensation will fool the fridge into thinking it has to defrost more often—and running the defrost cycle costs you extra money.

> Good free sources for covered food containers are empty margarine and cream cheese tubs, yogurt containers, sherbet tubs, and peanut butter jars.

Shopping Smart

196. Bartering is still alive and well.

Kiplinger's Personal Finance magazine estimates that over $880 million worth of goods and services were bartered last year through barter exchanges, organizations that trade in everything from dental work to home repairs. An exchange member pays the same fees as a cash customer but pays in "trade dollars," which the seller can take back to the exchange and later "spend." As of 1993, one community barter club in the college town of Ithaca, New York (Ithaca Money, Box 6578, Ithaca, NY 14851), logged over 2,000 hours' worth of transactions—the largest "purchase" so far was an eighteen-hour carpentry job. To find a barter exchange in your area, send a self-addressed stamped envelope to each of the two national groups covering this area of the economy: The National Association of Trade Exchanges, 9797 SW Tembrook, Portland, OR 97224, and the Reciprocal Trade Association, 9513 Beach Mill Road, Great Falls, VA 22066.

197. Catalogs offer good-value kids' clothing.

If you have kids, one catalog you definitely will not want to be without is Olsen's Mill Direct, which is the direct mill outlet for the popular and well-made Osh-Kosh B'Gosh lines of children's wear. Besides the overalls for which they are justly famous, the catalog also includes jumpers, shorts, hats, and even socks. An added bonus is the Carter's line of all-cotton underwear. Here is

Bartering sounds great, but is an exchange of goods and services taxable? *Kiplinger's* asked the IRS to comment on whether barter exchanges are a taxable event. The conclusion: If you trade services in your line of work—that is, an attorney writes a will for an accountant and the accountant keeps the attorney's books—then you're supposed to declare the fair-market value of the services as income on a form 1099-B. The trade associations mentioned in tip 196 can help give you specific information and procedures for staying on the right side of the IRS when you barter.

an opportunity to buy a superior product at a good price. Contact Olsen's Mill at 1641 South Main Street, Oshkosh, WI 54901 (1-800-537-4979). Or request catalogs from Lands' End (Dodgeville, WI, 1-800-356-4444) and After the Stork (Albuquerque, NM, 1-800-333-KIDS). These offer classic, reasonably priced, mostly cotton clothing for kids that will last through several siblings' use.

198. Have a shopping strategy.

If you come back from a trip to the supermarket or drugstore exhausted and frazzled, you're not alone. Items in stores are often laid out so that the most commonly shopped-for staples—such as flour, bread, meat, fruit, and paper goods—are as far apart from each other as possible. This placement keeps you, the customer, in the store longer and forces you to scan entire aisles to find just a few items. Why do store designers do this? In the

When you find yourself wandering with "rapture of the aisles" (a condition similar to the "rapture of the deep" deep-sea divers get right before they die), snap out of it and head for the checkout counter immediately. You'll live to shop another day.

hopes that by staying longer and scanning more, you'll be encouraged to purchase more items, even ones you don't need. How can you combat this strategy? By having one of your own. Always go shopping with a list and always go up and down an aisle only once. Try to frequent the same store or stores so that you know where the items you want are located.

199. To market, to market . . . without the dear kids.

It's far easier to avoid impulse buys at the grocery store if you go shopping without your children, who generally are notorious at spotting a dozen things they can't live without. If your cupboards are bare and you simply must bring your young children along when you shop, limit them to one favorite item each that is not on your list.

200. Keep crucial files handy.

Religiously save all your receipts and warranties in a separate file for quick reference in case anything ever goes wrong with a major appliance or piece of electronic equipment. Keep the file in a handy place—the kitchen or family room—and throw the receipt in even before you unpack the purchase.

Losing a receipt for an expensive purchase can really hurt, especially since you won't be able to take advantage of the warranty without it. For example, if you buy a new television set that needs repairing within the first year or two, you'll have to shell out $80 if you don't have your receipt. (That's the average cost of repairing a 20-inch TV set, according to *Consumer Reports*.)

201. Who needs this?

Beware the "loss leader." The loss leader is an item a store marks down to a really good price—say 25 cents a pint for strawberries—in order to get you into the store. Once it has you there, it entices you to buy additional items at higher markups—say $2 a can for whipping cream—by placing them near the loss leader. You're supposed to get so excited about the berries you don't realize—or care—you're paying 40 percent more than normal for the cream to go with them.

202. Keep your rooms fresh for less.

Just because you're frugal doesn't mean you can't enjoy the little luxuries of life, such as potpourri. Dried flowers are a great way to freshen rooms, but pricey to keep replenishing. Get more life out of your potpourri by buying a small vial of rose oil (or wintergreen or sandalwood, whichever you prefer) from a drugstore or health food store. Put a few drops on a cotton ball, and shove the ball down into the potpourri so that you can smell it but not see it. Simply replenish the ball instead of the potpourri each time the scent wears off.

> Many farmer's markets offer for just a few dollars large one-pound bags of newly dried flowers in a variety of intriguing scents. Besides giving you much more for your money, these dried flowers are a lot fresher and more aromatic than the tiny bags you can buy in your supermarket or discount store.

203. Are large economy sizes more economical?

Use the unit pricing labels in supermarkets to figure out the best buys—or whip out your handy, ever-present pocket calculator to do the math yourself. This is the only reliable way to figure out if a larger-size package is really a bargain.

Unit pricing labels often confirm your common sense. For example, buying a ready-made graham cracker crust for a cheesecake or other dessert costs $3.76 a pound. A box of graham cracker crumbs is less pricey, at $2.90 a pound. The cheapest option of all is to buy a regular box of graham crackers at $2.19 a pound. You'll need to crush only half the crackers in the box and you can enjoy the rest for munching. (Here's a quick cracker-crushing method: Put several grahams in a large airtight plastic bag. Close the bag, and run a rolling pin over it several times until the crackers are completely crumbly.)

On the other hand, unit labels can be surprising. Larger sizes are not necessarily the better buy. We compared the small (14 ounce), medium (28 ounce), and extra-large (64 ounce) sizes of Heinz ketchup. We discovered that the smallest and largest size both cost $1.79 per quart. Strangely, the medium-size bottle was significantly more expensive; it was priced at $2.05 per quart!

Checking the labels also showed us the most expensive ketchup option of all: trendy new salsa ketchup, which is a whopping $3.42 per quart. If you relish spicy condiments, buying a bottle of plain ketchup and adding a dab of your own salsa at home is the truly frugal (and most sensible) thing to do.

204. Get the scoop on coupons.

Generic vs. coupons? Dedicated clippers still can't convince us that coupons are necessarily a good thing. Why? Because too often they get you to buy something that you wouldn't ordinarily purchase, such as all sorts of convenience foods and frozen desserts. Our rule of thumb is always to check out the generic or store-brand version of the item first—usually it's even lower-priced than the couponed item. On the other hand, some supermarket chains offer double or triple off on any coupons, which makes them a much more appealing deal. Ask around at your local stores to see if any of them are as generous.

205. Catalog bargains can be found close to home.

The best audio and video bargains—at 15 to 20 percent below list price—can usually be found in catalogs. An added benefit is that if the firm is located in another state, you can legally avoid

Sometimes you can get the catalog price without shopping the catalog. Just take the advertised price to a local store and ask the manager if he or she will match it. Managers in large chains may not have the power to negotiate, but smaller, owner-manager shops will. You'll end up paying the sales tax, but you'll gain access to a local repair shop, which may be worth it—*Consumer Reports* research indicates that one in five video recorders needs service at some point.

state sales tax, which on big-ticket items can take a hefty bite out of your equipment budget. But if you order through the mail, make sure you take this precaution first: Ask about a manufacturer's warranty. If the product doesn't come with one, you won't be able to get free service if it goes on the blink.

206. Sound advice for audiophiles.

High-tech electronic or audio equipment can be very expensive. A good mail order source for this sort of stuff at discount prices is DAK. A unique feature of this mail order firm is that it offers you a sort of price protection—if you find the product you purchased selling for less anywhere else within thirty days, DAK will reimburse you the difference in credit toward a future purchase. Contact DAK at 1-800-325-0800.

Other well-regarded catalog sources of audio, video, and computer equipment are J & R Computer World (1-800-221-8180) and Crutchfield, which is particularly strong on car stereos and home office equipment (1-800-955-3000 or 1-800-388-4655).

207. Don't just *shop* resale and consignment—*sell* through it too.

Recycle your own things. Either take the tax credit for a donation or, as is the usual practice, get a check or in-store credit for materials you have brought in. Darcie has purchased used baby gear and brought it back in to resell again when outgrown. The net effect was that she paid $5 for the use of an infant car seat. (Do make sure any baby equipment you buy meets current safety standards, though.)

208. Go shopping around your own house first.

Clean your garage, attic, basement, or apartment storage box at least twice a year and make note of and update a list of all the junk (or treasures) you have stored there. You wouldn't believe how many people end up buying things they already own. For example, when Darcie ruined her wok she went out and bought a new one, completely forgetting that she had two more she had received years ago as wedding gifts out in the garage. (Hey, what were two of them doing in the garage, anyhow? One of them should have been garage-saled long ago.)

209. Don't overlook those shipping costs.

If you're tantalized by glossy home furnishings catalogs, remember to check the shipping charges first if you're thinking about buying furniture or carpet by mail. In many cases when you figure in the transportation costs, you'll find it is cheaper to shop nearer home.

210. Be choosy when buying generics.

Know which generic or store labels to buy at the grocery store and which to avoid. You won't be saving money if you purchase generic food your kids refuse to eat—or no-name diapers that leak and soil your baby's clothes twice as often as the major brands. We like to look for President's Choice, a private-label brand sold in many supermarkets that has high-quality products for significantly lower prices than its better-known competitors. Its products range from the mundane, such as bottled juices, to the exotic, including green peppercorn Dijon mustard.

211. Who needs this?

Never buy juice boxes. Not only are they ecologically unsound, they're a terrible waste of money. Use reusable plastic sipper cups instead.

> **B**uying disposable drink boxes for your kids' lunch boxes costs around $4.40 a week, or $686 a year. On the other hand, you can get a Rubbermaid washable plastic drink box for $1.99 (or any other refillable plastic cup) and fill it up with your own juice to save more than $50 a year.

212. Save money generated from grocery store coupons.

You can pay your grocery store bill in full, then pocket the change received after the coupons are deducted. Keep the coupon money in a special place and let it accumulate each week. One family uses this money to buy Christmas presents—by saving all year in this painless way, they have saved enough by the time the holidays arrive. Another couple we know uses their "found money" from coupons to cover all their entertainment and dining expenses.

213. Savings on raisins.

Those small cardboard raisin boxes are handy to keep in the car or your bag, but you pay a premium for the packaging. Keep your convenience and your cash too by buying them from the supermarket only once. After their contents are eaten, reuse the boxes and fill them with raisins purchased in bulk. These are a good treat to carry around with you when "snack attacks" strike your kids—or you.

A big 15-ounce box of raisins costs $1.79, which adds up to $1.91 a pound. A package of those small boxes, which weighs a scant 9 ounces, will cost you $1.59—for an actual cost of $2.38 a pound. So the bigger box saves you 50 cents. An even better buy would be a 24-ounce canister of raisins at $2.79, which would end up costing you only $1.86 a pound.

214. Charge it.

Buy rechargeable batteries for radios, toys, and other battery-eaters. The savings are significant in the long run.

One study by *Money* magazine found that a battery-powered cassette player would go through 876 alkaline batteries in three years, for a total cost of $657. But using rechargeable batteries would cost only $26 for the same period of time, even when you factor in the cost of the recharger and electricity. So you would come out $631 ahead, as well as having the satisfaction of knowing that you didn't contribute to any landfill problems by throwing away all those used batteries!

215. Buy in bulk only when it makes sense.

A good way to do this is to join a food co-op or warehouse club. Food co-ops also can be a great source of organic and natural foods. But be choosy about what you stock up on. It's a good idea to buy oil by the case at a discount store, and a whole year's supply is not that difficult to find storage space for. But unless you have a huge freezer or plenty of friends to share with, buying a whole year's worth of meat or cheese is not nearly as sensible.

For instance, our local club offers 5 pounds of honey for $1.15. This is a great buy compared to $1.65 for a measly little 12-ounce jar at the supermarket, and it's easy to store too. If you've got a large pantry and several kids who love pb & j sandwiches, 40 pounds of peanut butter for $65 is also a swell bargain. But unless you've got a huge freezer, whole turkeys at 39 cents a pound might not be an item you want to stock up on in huge quantities.

> **D**iscount warehouse clubs, such as BJ's (1-800-257-2582) and Sam's (1-800-925-6278), make sense only if you stick to the staples (paper goods, cereal, canned goods) that are their stock in trade. Though you also can find office equipment and furniture at these places, the prices are not nearly so good, and the salespeople are not knowledgeable about these bigger-ticket items.

216. Cut carpet costs.

When shopping for carpet, march right past the floor displays and head for the back. Ask to see the remainder rolls, which are the last six to twenty feet of carpet that stores usually move off the shop floor to make room for full rolls. These rolls are not "seconds"—they are not returns or damaged in any way—yet typically they sell for 20 to 40 percent less than carpet cut from the full rolls out on the display floor. You may have to try several stores to find a remnant that suits you and is the appropriate size, but at these savings it's time well spent.

Darcie and Lenny recently got some very nice gray carpet for their bedroom for $12.95 a yard by taking a remnant. The original roll had sold for $19.95 a yard. They had about two feet left over, which Darcie's dad immediately commandeered for floor mats for his van.

217. Pick frozen juice.

Frozen juice is almost half the cost of ready-made juice sold in bottles or cartons. Our local grocery store charges $2.25 for a quart of ready-made OJ, as opposed to their $1.29 bargain price on a frozen canister that makes one and a half quarts. If you used to buy two cartons of juice a week, but switch to buying frozen juice canisters, you'll save $100 a year without giving up anything. Juice kept in glass bottles also loses many of its vitamins (and taste) when exposed to the light, so it's not even as good for you as the kind you dilute yourself. (For young children, add an extra can of water to cut down on the amount of sugar they're taking in, for a 25 percent savings on every jar you mix up.)

218. Be ready to make returns.

Even if you pride yourself on being a savvy shopper, it's likely that several times a year you make an inappropriate purchase, such as a sweater that really doesn't match the slacks you had in mind, or the wrong kind of paper for your printer. The frugal thing to do, of course, is to return the item for a refund, but in order to do that you have to remember to do two things at the time of purchase—not after. First, always check the return policy for your items, since requirements vary greatly. Some stores will accept returns for only seven days after a purchase, others for as many as thirty. Some will only make exchanges, not refunds. And second, keep your receipt. Your itemized receipt is usually a must for a refund, though some stores will allow an exchange without one. If you pay by credit card, have the sales clerk staple the itemized receipt directly onto the credit card slip—that way they won't get separated.

219. Always ask the salesperson, "Can you do better?"

Negotiate whenever you buy a large-ticket item, such as an appliance or electronic equipment, not just when you're buying a car. If you don't ask for a better deal, you'll never know if you could have gotten a better price. If you do ask, you may be pleasantly surprised how accommodating salespeople can be if they want to make a sale. This tactic is often less successful at large department stores, which have rigid sales policies, so try bargaining in smaller stores.

Darcie is lucky enough to know a semiprofessional shopper, her brother-in-law Eric. People beg Eric to go with them on shopping trips for everything from cars to air conditioners. He always gets them a better deal. Here are Eric's top two tips for negotiating deals with salesmen.

Tip 1: Don't shop in the store that's having a sale. Why? Because the best you'll get is the sale price. Go to the *competitor* of the store that's having a sale and say, "The air conditioner you're selling for $600 is on sale for $520 at Tops across town. I'm in your store right now. Can you do better? How about $480?"

Tip 2: Always have a comeback line. If, for instance, the air-conditioner salesman says, "Well, I can match Tops' price but not go lower," then you say, "I work around the corner from Tops and can pick up my air conditioner at that $520 price very easily. Tell you what—how about if I split the difference with you?" More often than not, the salesman will go confer with his manager and come back with an offer of $500.

220. Who needs this?

Instead of choosing a 10½-ounce package of microwave popcorn, which costs around $2.50 (and is coated with oil you might not want in your diet), you can buy 2 pounds of plain popcorn kernels for about 69 cents. A hot air popper will set you back under $20 and pay for itself in just two months. If you use a bag of microwave popcorn a week, the hot air popper will save you close to $200 a year. At savings like this, popping it yourself is simply smarter. Plus, making air-popped corn is more entertaining than watching a paper bag spin around.

221. Buy name-brand food through outlets.

Most of us have explored clothing outlet stores and found some bargains there—but did you know that you can also buy well-known brands of food through outlet stores? In the Chicago area alone you can buy wonderful desserts or large trays of lasagna and other entrées from a Sara Lee outlet, fresh bread and crackers at a Pepperidge Farm outlet, and other bread and bakery items at a Holsom Bread outlet. (At Holsom, in fact, you can get two loaves of bread and one bag each of hot dog and hamburger buns for just over $2!) Search your Yellow Pages under the type of store and the "Outlets" listing, or keep your eyes open for similar stores in your area.

222. Get your medicine through the mail.

If you have a prescription that doesn't need to be filled immediately, try using one of the mail order pharmacies, which offer discounts up to 40 percent. Two reliable ones recommended by *Money* magazine are Action Mail Order (1-800-452-1976) and Family Pharmaceuticals (1-800-922-3444).

In our experience, the discounts are good but don't apply across the board. For instance, we were quoted $20 for 60 caps of the estrogen replacement drug Premarin—that's $1 more expensive than our local pharmacy charges! On the other hand, for another drug, the generic version of the heart medication Tenormin, the mail order discount was a whopping 50 percent ($7 versus $14). The moral is: Get a local quote first to make sure you're really getting one of deep-discounted mail order deals.

AARP (the American Association of Retired Persons) offers its members good discount prices on prescription drugs, over-the-counter medications, and medical supplies, such as walkers and elastic stockings. Although senior citizens get the best discounts, you don't need to be over fifty to order drugs from AARP's pharmacy service. Contact it at AARP, 1909 K Street NW, Washington, DC 20049 (1-800-283-3310 or 1-800-456-4636) to request a catalog.

223. Don't get conned by convenience.

We recently priced two kinds of Parmesan at our local supermarket. The name-brand canister of pregrated cheese costs around $3.49 for 8 ounces, while fresh Parmesan costs $3.99 for a full pound—that's almost half the price of the prepackaged variety. Fresh Parmesan also has a much tastier, livelier flavor. If you ask nicely, the deli department might even grate the cheese for you. Our deli manager told us that if you double-bag the fresh grated Parmesan and store it in your freezer, it will keep almost indefinitely.

224. Don't be a patsy for packaging.

Those cute little mini Ritz crackers, teddy bear cookies, and other tiny snacks have two major problems: They cost nearly twice as much per ounce as regular-size snacks, and people tend to munch large handfuls of them at a time. (They're so small they

A quick trip to the supermarket with the calculator revealed Salerno Dinosaur Grahams selling at $2.29 for a 13-ounce package, while the Mini Dinos were priced at $1.99 for a 10-ounce bag. Don't be fooled by the lower price for the smaller bag—the Minis are actually 36 cents a pound more expensive than the full-size grahams.

must not have any calories to speak of, right?) We suggest sticking to the old standbys of raisins and popcorn. Or you can always make up a batch of teeny little cookies next time you bake by dropping dough onto the baking sheet by the half-teaspoonful instead of using a teaspoon or tablespoon.

225. Buy your computer through the mail.

If you're in the market for a home (or home-office) computer, consult the ads in the back of the most popular computer magazines. Several mail order companies advertise computer equipment closeouts—often you can find these deals under the heading "Very Limited Supply." Before you worry about whether these computers are still in good shape, you should know that some of them have never been out of their boxes. They just have the misfortune to be discontinued models, even though they're brand new and in mint condition. If you don't subscribe to the computer-world theory that anything over a year old is hopelessly outmoded, you can get some terrific bargains. Martha's family recently bought a color monitor for their Macintosh this way and saved $150 off the list price for that model. The low-end monitor they bought is no longer on the market, so their savings are even higher when you consider that the current model costs $600 more than the price they paid.

226. Smart buys save money.

Do your homework before making any large purchases. The time you spend will save you money in the end. One of our friends swears by *Consumer Reports* magazine (back issues of which are usually available in your public library). She and her husband scour back issues every time they're in the market for an appliance, audio equipment, or a new car. They bought their brand of VCR because it had the lowest repair rate of any VCR the magazine tested. So far, they've had it for eight years and it's worked flawlessly, even though it's never been cleaned and their three-

Shopping by mail can be a bargain, but watch out for the hidden shipping costs. Many suppliers pass the shipping costs on to the customer, and depending on distance and weight, these charges can come awfully close to the $100 you may save on the list price. Always ask for the estimated shipping charges when comparing prices. If something is defective with a unit and you have to return it, that cost will be entirely yours. So, as usual, buyer beware.

year-old son has a habit of putting tapes in backward or upside down. By contrast, some of our friends' coworkers were complaining that they've had their VCR in the shop several times in five years. This shopping method is not infallible, of course, but reading the product reviews carefully is a good place to start before you shop. Since having your VCR cleaned and repaired can cost between $50 and $90, you can save that much each year by buying the right model to begin with.

227. Cash in on a rain check.

If you dash over to a discount store advertising a terrific deal on lawn furniture, chain saws, or whatever, and arrive to find the shelves are completely bare, don't gnash your teeth and lament the loss of your savings—just ask for a rain check. Many stores will give you a coupon enabling you to purchase an item at its sale price when it comes back in stock. Driving back to the store can be well worth the effort if it's a good enough discount and if you don't desperately need to buy the item that day.

228. Another freebie.

Set up an informal coupon exchange to make the most of your clipping. We come across a lot of coupons for products our families don't want or need. For months, Darcie traded diaper coupons with her sister in New Jersey (Huggies for Pampers) and traded cat food for cookie coupons with relatives in Florida. The more people in your exchange, the bigger the pool of products you'll have to choose from. In some communities the local library or senior center sets up a coupon exchange box—see if your community center or a group you belong to may be willing to embark on this project. It's a valuable community service that can be provided at no cost and with no extra personnel.

> **M**aterials needed for a community coupon exchange box: four or five empty shoe boxes and a Magic Marker. Label the short end of each box with the appropriate letters to alphabetize the contents (A–F, G–M, etc.) and you're in business. If the exchange is going on a bulletin board instead of a table, use large manila envelopes instead.

229. Get your money back on bad buys.

In our experience, if you're a consumer, you've got a complaint about something, whether it's bait-and-switch advertising, misrepresentation of warranties, or a shoddy repair job. Hey, we all love to complain, but to whom? (We disqualify coworkers and that guy in line behind you at the supermarket—their sympathy is questionable and their ability actually to do something about it is nil.) If you want to do something about it, call the National Fraud Information Center at 1-800-876-7060. This service, which is run by the National Consumer's League of Washington, D.C., provides background information on your rights as a consumer and then can refer you to the proper authority in your area to take action.

Is it worth complaining? You bet. Over the past four years we've had a CD player ($120), a water softener ($600), a cordless phone ($90), a car seat ($45), and an electrical service upgrade ($500) either replaced or reserviced by complaining.

Another handy toll-free number you might want to know about is the Consumer Product Safety Commission's Hotline: 1-800-638-CPSC. The Safety Commission offers recorded messages on all consumer products that have been recalled within the past ninety days.

230. Want the dirt on those dirt-cheap ads?

You've probably seen them in the back of magazines and newspapers, offering information on buying surplus from the government "dirt cheap." The only catch is that they charge you for the information. Well, the government will send you information on its auctions absolutely free if you write to them at the Consumer Information Center, Pueblo, CO 81009 and request booklets on federal government sales.

Be warned that government surplus is often just that—junk that federal and state agencies have already rejected and sent on to the auction centers. The much-advertised luxury items seized on drug raids—cars, houses, and jewelry in very questionable taste—sell at special auctions at fair-market value. Good buys can sometimes be found at the post office when unclaimed goods are sold. Contact your local post office to find out the time and location of its next sale. And many local police stations hold sales of abandoned cars, motorcycles, and bicycles.

231. Shop at the right time.

Do you like busy, crowded stores with surly, overworked clerks and lines a mile long in front of every checkout counter? Then do your shopping on Fridays and Saturdays, which are, according to the International Mass Retail Association, the favorite shopping days of most people.

In contrast, savvy frugal shoppers prefer doing their marketing and errands on the least busy days: Monday and Tuesday. Why? Because then they have time to query clerks on special deals and warranties, bargain down managers, compare costs, and zip through the checkout lines. And, since Americans spend an average of $1.33 per minute at the supermarket, getting through the store as quickly as you can will save you a significant amount of money.

Always try to spend the least amount of time in the checkout line as possible, because stores usually place every impulse-buy item imaginable near you at that point. If you're shopping with young children, the array of candy and gum can be especially problematical. Here is where your pocket calculator comes in handy—try to distract the youngsters by having them add up the groceries and "beat" the clerk.

232. Read that register tape.

Don't forget to check prices carefully while your purchases are being rung up, both at the grocery store and at shopping centers. You'll be surprised how often the wrong price is entered, even with all those fancy key codes on everything. Sale prices are the ones to scrutinize most closely, since the prices in the computer may not be up to date. For example, in one shopping excursion the other day, Martha was overcharged at two different stores. A clothing store charged her $29.95 for a pair of jeans even though the label read $24.95, and the local bookstore neglected to give her a 30 percent discount on a best-selling paperback. In both cases, the cashiers quickly refunded the money as soon as Martha pointed out the problem. If she didn't have the habit of checking her receipts, she would have lost $7.75 that day.

Managing Your Money, Mortgage, Investments, and Insurance

233. Smart buys save money.

Purchase a small cheap hand calculator (many can be found for under $5 in drugstores) and carry it everywhere with you to help you compare costs, check quotes for services, and double-check percentage discounts.

234. Pare down your property taxes.

If you've been in your home a long time and watched with dismay as houses selling around yours drive your property tax up and up, here's good news: Nineteen states and the District of Columbia offer tax programs whereby you can opt to defer property tax payments until after your death or the sale of your house. In the event of your death, the state gets its money from your estate.

Typically there are age or income requirements for this program, which vary state by state. If you are lucky enough to live in one of the states with such a program, check with your local tax assessor's office for more details; if your state doesn't have this program, call up your local state representatives and ask them why not.

States offering property tax deferral programs: California, Colorado, District of Columbia, Florida, Georgia, Illinois, Iowa, Maine, Maryland, Massachusetts, Michigan, New Hampshire, North Dakota, Oregon, Tennessee, Texas, Utah, Virginia, Washington, and Wisconsin.

235. Smart buys save money.

If you've recently spent some hard-earned cash to improve your home security with smoke detectors, deadbolt door locks, or outdoor lighting, spend an extra 25 cents and call your insurance agent. In many cases improved security will qualify you for a discount on your homeowner's insurance premium.

236. Buy bonds direct.

Treasury bonds are still a great secure investment, but paying big brokerage fees can really cut into the profit you make from them. The good news is that you can buy them directly from the government—but only at certain auction times. For instructions on how and when to buy from the government, write Treasury Direct, Bureau of Public Debt, Department F, Washington, DC 20239.

237. Say "No thanks" to the bank.

If you're getting tired of banks that keep increasing their service fees (and cutting their services), look into joining a credit union. Credit unions usually offer higher rates on money market and savings accounts, and lower rates on car and personal loans. They even offer credit cards with fairly reasonable interest rates! We recommend that you use credit unions for loans, but not for savings, since credit union savings deposits are not insured by the FDIC. Our local credit union offers a personal loan at 9.9 percent for two years. Our bank, on the other hand, has a 12.4 percent variable rate on personal loans. Going with the credit union can save you hundreds of dollars over the life of your loan.

Credit union memberships have been increasing steadily—there are more than 13,000 nationally with nearly 64 million members. Many corporations offer their employees access to a credit union—or call the Credit Union National Association at 1-800-358-5710 to get more information.

238. Picture this . . . and this . . . and this. . . .

Minimize your losses in the event of theft, fire, or flood. Keep an inventory of all your possessions for insurance purposes. If you already own a videocamera, the easiest thing to do is simply go from room to room videotaping all your stuff. (Don't forget the garage, basement, attic, etc.) This way there'll be no question of replacement value in the event of fire, theft, or water damage. If you're not quite that high tech, use your regular camera instead to take a variety of photos throughout the house. Don't forget to redo your tape or photos every few years after you've accumulated more "stuff," and remember to store the tape or pictures outside your own home, with a relative or in a safety deposit box.

239. How good is your banker's math?

According to one government study, pretty poor when it comes to figuring the changes in your ARM (adjustable rate mortgage). A study of 7,000 ARMs found rate-adjustment errors in half of them. Your lender also could be missing discounts due you for early tax payments. Two commercial companies will check your mortgage adjustments for you for a fee: LoanTech (301-762-7700) and LoanCheck (619-578-5224). You can usually clear matters up by calling your lender's loan servicing department and reviewing the paperwork. Make sure the math is right and that your increase is tied to the correct index as specified in your original mortgage papers.

If you're planning to move in a couple of years, refinancing might pay anyway. Just go for a low-rate adjustable loan instead of a fixed rate mortgage. The first year or two of adjustable rates can be well below 5 percent, making this a very smart choice for people on the move. When shopping for a new mortgage, also look for banks offering no-points deals on refinancing.

240. Cut the garbage fees on your mortgage in half.

When buying or selling a house, negotiate closing costs. Those ridiculous notary, research, document, and transfer charges that come with your mortgage (commonly known as "garbage fees") usually add up to $400 to $500. Usually you can't negotiate with your bank to get rid of them, because this is where the lenders make their money. Don't give up, though—you might have better luck with the seller or the real estate agents. As parties interested in seeing the sale go through, they can be approached for a 50/50 split on the fees.

Though certain expenses traditionally fall to the buyer or the seller, if you have very hungry buyers (or desperate sellers) there may be room for improvement. Our old neighbors had to move because the wife was transferred to another city. They were so eager to sell that they paid for all the buyers' document and transfer fees.

241. Is it time to refinance?

Everyone knows that the conventional wisdom is to refinance your home if the *new* interest rate will be more than ½ to 1 point *below* what you are currently paying. When exploring this option, don't forget to figure in the closing costs—a little quick math may indicate that the time isn't right. If you plan to stay in your house at least two more years, which is long enough to make the closing costs worthwhile, refinancing is probably well worth it. You may even be able to cut your monthly payments by 25 percent or so if you took out a mortgage a few years ago when rates were over 10 or 12 percent.

242. Take control of your credit cards.

Carry, use, and pay off completely each month only one credit card—it will help you resist the temptation to play round robin with cards and thereby incur some of the most expensive interest charges in the history of the universe. However, if you're married and have no credit cards in your name, do apply for one or two new cards on your own to establish that all-important credit history.

> Refusing to carry credit card debt saves you double money—first, the cost of the item itself, and second, the financing charge. For example, say you decide not to put a new $300 TV on your card. Assuming your card carries 16 percent interest, you have actually saved $348. If you really really really want that new tube, then follow the other recommendations in this book. You can easily save $100 a month for the next three months and then buy that TV for cash. You still will have saved $48—and you'll have the TV too!

243. Another freebie.

Get free help analyzing or comparing insurance policies from the National Insurance Consumer Organization (NICO). This is an easy way to ensure you are getting the best coverage at the best cost. Contact NICO at 121 North Payne Street, Alexandria, VA 22314, or call the toll-free number (1-800-942-4242) to get answers to your questions on property and liability insurance.

244. Protect your stuff.

Don't forget to get personal property insurance if you're a renter. Apartments as well as houses get burgled or damaged by fire and water. It will cost around $100 a year to get $25,000 worth of property coverage at full replacement value if you live in a suburban area; property insurance in urban areas will be more expensive.

245. Think before buying air travel insurance.

No matter how much "insurance" you buy, none of it will *ensure* that the plane won't crash! (If you have such a strong premonition that the flight will crash, take Amtrak instead.) The only time travel insurance can be useful is if you're buying an expensive nonrefundable travel package, such as a cruise. Most trip cancellation and interruption insurance policies cost around $5 or $5.50 per $100 of coverage. If you have to cancel your cruise at the last minute because of a family illness, having the insurance pay you back is much better than losing several thousand dollars.

246. Go low.

Choose mutual funds with low "expense ratios"—the portion of profit that the firm takes for managing the fund portfolio. The average is about 1.25 percent of the fund's value, so look for funds with less than that. (Read the prospectus to learn about a fund's operating expenses.) In general, short- and limited-term government bond funds are less expensive to operate than longer-term bond funds; fixed income funds are cheaper to manage than equity (stock) funds; and overseas funds cost more to manage than U.S. mutual funds.

If you're comfortable with managing your own investments, look for no-load funds that don't have a hefty commission fee when you buy or sell them. Several magazines, such as *Forbes,*

Money, and *Kiplinger's Personal Finance,* offer annual mutual fund performance surveys. Check your library or newsstand for their recommendations on which funds to buy.

If you don't know much about mutual fund investing, you might want to choose a "level load" fund instead. That's a no-load fund you can buy through an investment advisor. It'll cost a trifle more to purchase—but if your advisor steers you to winning funds that consistently perform well, that small charge will be well worth it. When buying through an investment firm, look for "back-load" funds for long-term investments. A back-load fund manager will take 5 percent of your investment if you pull out within a year. But if you hold on to your investment for five years or longer, you won't have to pay a fee at all. "Front-load" funds, on the other hand, grab a portion of your money as soon as you invest it.

247. Bypass brokers.

If you do want to buy stocks, how can you totally avoid those nasty brokerage fees that cut into your profits? Implement a DRIP, or dividend reinvestment program. A DRIP allows you to bypass commission fees when you purchase additional shares of stock you already own. Not every company offers this feature to shareholders, so don't forget to ask this question before buying a stock you fancy. Not only do DRIPs offer a convenient way to buy additional shares of stock without brokerage fees, they also give you the option of taking some of your dividends in cash.

The American Association of Individual Investors publishes an annual listing of companies that offer DRIP plans ($10 for nonmembers). You can get more information by contacting the AAII at 625 N. Michigan Avenue, Suite 1900, Chicago, IL 60611; 312-280-0170.

248. Make all your investment money work for you.

While more than one hundred stocks allow *existing* shareholders to purchase additional shares directly, more and more companies have started letting individuals make an *initial* investment on their own without a broker. Since many brokers' minimum fees are $60 per transaction, setting up even the smallest portfolio through one of them can cost you several hundred dollars. Do it yourself and let all your investment money end up in your pocket. Four major corporations offer shares directly to the public in all states: Exxon, Texaco, Atmos Energy Corp., and Johnson Controls.

249. Who needs this?

Never carry a credit card that charges an annual fee. It's silly to pay a $50 to $60 fee each year if you don't have to. Shop around for a credit card without an annual fee. Since you pay off your balance completely each month (right?), you don't care if the interest rate is higher. *Money* magazine regularly compares cards and fees nationwide—go to your local library and look up a back issue to get this information.

250. Get a fifteen-year mortgage at a thirty-year rate.

Take out a thirty-year mortgage, but still make some extra payments toward your principal each month for big savings over the life of your loan. Prepaying like this can be smarter than locking yourself into a fifteen-year mortgage, since you may not be able to swing the higher payments that come with the shorter term, especially if you lose your job or experience another kind of financial crisis.

251. Get a jump on tax planning.

Instead of celebrating the day after Thanksgiving with a shopping spree, sit down with your copy of last year's tax form and make a rough estimate of this year's taxes to see if you are falling short of

Accelerating your payment schedule on your own can make a serious dent in the amount of interest you pay the bank over the life of your mortgage. For example, paying $100 extra a month on a 7 percent loan of $100,000 will cut your payment period by a full third, down to only 20 years. Assuming $7,000 a year in interest payments, you have just saved $70,000. Even just $50 a month extra will keep about six years' worth of interest payments in your pockets instead of the bank's coffers.

qualifying for any deductibles—such as medical expenses or dependent care—that you want to qualify for. That will give you a month to make legitimate tax-planning adjustments, such as moving up a scheduled surgery or paying January's rent in December.

252. Rebid your house and car insurance every year.

Many people do a good job of shopping only the first time they buy insurance and then automatically write that premium check twice a year forever. Meanwhile, your possessions are changing, the house is being improved, the age and status of your vehicles are changing, and insurance companies offer new programs with things like incentives for covering both your house and car with the same firm. Rebid every year! We saved $200 on insurance last year when we realized we were still automatically carrying collision on a ten-year-old car whose Blue Book value had slipped below the deductible! (Of course, we kept full liability to protect ourselves.)

253. Pare down your property taxes.

Visit your local tax assessor to make sure you are not being overcharged on your property taxes. Their information on your property is often incorrect. For instance, our neighbors were being assessed $1,200 for a fireplace, when what they really have is a wood-burning stove. These stoves are not assessed at all, since they are considered to be part of the house's heating equipment and not a luxury item. Their tax bill went down after this mistake was corrected.

254. Who needs this?

Never buy credit insurance, which pays off any car or mortgage loans if you were to become disabled or die before paying off the loan. This can cost an additional $300 on a $10,000 car or personal loan. You can insure yourself for this problem via your disability or life insurance policy.

255. Insure your stuff for enough.

Get "replacement" coverage for your house's contents instead of "actual cash value," which declines quickly over time. Some policies will give you that coverage automatically. If not, you can get replacement value coverage for $50,000 worth of your household belongings starting from a mere $25 to $35 (depending on your home's location and the size of your deductible).

256. Who needs this?

Never even *think* about playing your state lottery. For example, the odds against winning the Illinois State Lotto are 12,900,000 to 1. If you enjoy gambling, invest in the stock market instead. You'll have a much better chance of getting lucky. Often you can do well if you buy stock in a company that makes products that your family regularly buys and enjoys. (Martha's family bought Walt Disney stock because their kids and all their children's friends have tons of Disney tapes, books, costumes, stuffed animals, and so on. So far, this investment has done quite well.)

257. Cancel your insurance.

Your mortgage insurance, that is. If you put less than 20 percent down on your house or condo, your lender probably required you to buy mortgage insurance. This is the most wasteful insurance you can buy, since it benefits the bank, not you. But once equity in your home reaches the 20 percent mark, mortgage insurance usually is no longer required. Of course, it may not cross your lender's corporate mind to inform you of this, so submit a request in writing to see if you are eligible to drop the mortgage insurance. If you are still worried about your family meeting the payments in event of death or disability, increase your life and disability coverage instead—that money is paid directly to you.

258. Don't tempt the tax man.

There are plenty of armchair accountants out there offering tax tips, and recently Darcie's husband ran into one at work. The advice was to lower the withholding amount on his paycheck in order to increase the amount of cash available to him in his paycheck each month. It sounded great—after all, why should the government make interest on our money instead of us? Still, Martha suggested we check with an accountant friend, and she was right—the accountant warned us about the IRS's Underpayment Penalty. This penalty can run $500 or more and is levied against you if you have not withheld either 100 percent of last year's tax liability or 90 percent of this year's estimated amount. Ouch! What's the use of keeping an extra $50 a month if you have to pay out double that in penalty fees come April 15?

Want to figure out how much you can legally withhold without incurring the penalty? Call the IRS at 1-800-829-3676 and request publication 919, "Is My Withholding Correct?" This nifty little brochure is revised every year to reflect the current tax tables and is much, much, much easier to use and more specific than the W-4 forms usually circulated by your employer.

259. Are ATMS A-OK?

Not if they cost you money every time you use them. If you don't pay attention to your bank's rules about ATM usage, you may be shocked to discover hefty fees for ATM transactions on your next bank statement. Many banks used to offer this service for free but have recently changed their policies. Martha's bank is typical—it offered unlimited ATM access when she first opened her savings account. Then it switched to a maximum of eight free ATM transactions a month. A few months ago the bank manager suddenly declared that there would be a $1 fee every time a customer uses another bank's ATM. Needless to say, Martha now makes all her withdrawals from her bank's own ATMs—and is looking around for another bank with more customer-friendly practices. Do remember to read all of your bank's fine print about your accounts. ATMs may be more convenient, but they're not worth paying extra for the privilege of using them.

260. Insure yourself inexpensively.

If you, your family, or your small group is shopping for the lowest premiums for life insurance, health insurance, and annunities, consider joining an insurance price-comparison service such as Quotesmith (1-800-556-9393). For their $35 annual membership fee you get unlimited rate quotes from more than 350 insurance companies, including Blue Cross and Blue Shield. If you buy several types of insurance each year, the service can really be worth it. Or you can pay $15 and ask Quotesmith to recommend several insurers for one particular type of policy. On a recent quote on life insurance for a thirty-year-old woman, the service revealed a range in premiums from $120 to $200. It also will provide information on the lowest cost for buying your insurance over a five- or ten-year period.

261. Another freebie.

When is a tax-free investment worth it to you, and when should you go for the usually higher yields of taxable investment vehicles? Franklin Mutual Funds is offering a free tax-yield calculator. (It looks like those slide rules you were never able to master in college, except that this is one you actually can figure out.) This tax rule can translate tax-free into taxable yields to provide you with the answer in a flash. Call 1-800-342-5236 and order yours now, before Congress changes the tax code again.

262. A freebie from the IRS!

Sure, the IRS provides a great free service with its Taxpayer Question Hot Line (1-800-829-1040), but it's a victim of its own success—so many people use it you may not be able to get through. Still, who wouldn't rather get expert advice for free, instead of spending $100 or more on a tax preparation accountant?

To increase your chances of getting a human instead of a busy signal, avoid calling on Mondays—that's when the line is the busiest due to weekend tax warriors calling up with all the problems they ran into when they sat down and tried to do their taxes on Sunday.

Don't take advantage of another IRS service, however—electronic filing. This sounds like a great convenience for people who fill out their tax returns using tax software on their home computers. You'll pay dearly for this convenience, though—it costs $20 to $40 to have your return filed electronically. We'll stick with using paper tax forms and a 29-cent stamp, thank you.

263. Bank by mail.

For your checks, that is. Mail order discounters such as Checks in the Mail (1-800-733-4443) and Current (1-800-533-3973) charge you only about half of what your bank does for checks. You can buy 200 imprinted checks for a mere $4.95 to $6.95. Or, if you or a friend owns a computer and printer, consider splitting the cost of one of the numerous check-printing programs to create your own.

264. Get rid of duplicate insurance.

Of course, everyone tells you to do this, but unless you actually sit down once a year to review all your policies together (home, health, and car), you might not catch the duplicates. We suggest January 1 as a good review date. The first place to check is the medical area of your auto policy—very often your health insurance policy already covers accidents and hospitalization. You can save around $30 a year just by canceling that unneeded medical coverage.

265. Check up on your credit.

You don't want to lose out on a good mortgage rate or new car loan because of a bad credit report. If you have the information in hand before your lender does, you can take the necessary steps to clear up your record. (Send a letter of explanation about any errors in your report, and start paying off your legitimate debts.) For a free copy of your credit report, send your name, address, social security number, and a copy of your driver's license or phone bill to: TRW Consumer Assistance (1-800-682-7654). You also can contact Trans Union at 1-800-851-2674.

266. Get a discount with your dividends.

While about 1,000 companies offer dividend reinvestment plans (DRIP), only 100 or so offer the extra incentive of a discount to shareholders participating in the DRIP. Discount DRIPs are nothing to scoff at—combined with your zero cost for brokerage fees, they allow you to make an automatic profit every time you reinvest. For more information on discount DRIP companies, consult *Buying Stocks Without a Broker* by Charles Carlson (McGraw-Hill).

Companies offering a 5 percent discount on shares purchased with reinvested dividends include: Bancorp Hawaii, First of America Bank, Kemper Insurance, and Piedmont Natural Gas. American Express offers a 3 percent discount.

267. Go for the gold.

If you qualify for a gold MasterCard or Visa, and you manage to find one with a low annual fee, grab it. (A little detective work can turn up some good credit card deals. Colonial National Bank USA, for example, offers a Gold Visa card with no annual fee and an annual percentage rate of 12.9 percent.) Many gold cards offer terrific additional benefits, including automatic travel accident insurance, collision and loss damage insurance when you rent a car, and extended warranties on large purchases. If your credit card has this last feature, you can double the one-year warranty on electronic equipment and other new items you buy without any effort on your part.

268. Give in to the urge to splurge—in a frugal sort of way, of course.

Every evening, empty your pocket change into an old coffee can or teapot. At the end of the month, take whatever is in the can and spend it on something absolutely frivolous and nonessential. Having a little spree like this to look forward to can help you save on the big stuff all month long.

In the Classroom

Teaching and Learning

269. Cut college costs.

Students can save up to 25 percent (including housing, food, and tuition) by finishing undergraduate school in three years instead of four. Start planning early—high school seniors can earn extra credits for college by taking special Advanced Placement classes. Once your children are in college, they can take summer classes during the regular school year. Make sure they get independent study credit for any jobs or internships they might hold. With good planning anyone can graduate in three and a half years. With a little persistence students can get out a whole year early and hit the job market on the run.

Two colleges recently launched formal three-year degree programs: Drury College in Springfield, Missouri, and Albertus Magnus College in New Haven, Connecticut. For more information on their programs, contact their admissions departments.

270. Save on SAT prep.

Every year thousands of parents plunk down hundreds of dollars apiece to put their high school children through SAT cram courses. (Some SAT tutors in New York charge as much as $300 an hour for their expertise!) Now there's a board game called Test Taking

Advantage available from the National Association of Secondary School Principals that features questions similar to those on the SAT test. It has ten categories of playing cards with questions on math, grammar, analogy, and reading comprehension, all presented within the context of a game that makes studying fun. To order, call NASSP at 1-800-253-7746. The cost is $44.95, which isn't cheap for a game, but it's a downright bargain for a cram course.

271. Another freebie.

Do you want to help your kids get on the right track with science and math, even though you are unsure of your own skills as a tutor? Before you sign up for expensive outside help, consider the free booklet from the U.S. Department of Education called "Helping Your Child Learn Science." This fifty-eight-page publication contains easy-to-do science experiments that you and your kids ages three to ten can do at home with commonly found household objects. For instance, there's one nice physics experiment that teaches about the principles of inertia and momentum with a raw potato and paper straws. You can order the booklet by writing to Department 611X, Consumer Information Center, Pueblo, CO 81009. You also can request a booklet titled "Science Fair Projects" by contacting the National Reference Service, Library of Congress, Washington, DC 20540 (202-707-5522).

272. Be a senior scholar.

Here's one way to go back to school for more education yourself, even if you're short on the cash to do it. Orville Redenbacher's new Second Start Scholarship Program is specifically designed for students over the age of thirty and provides awards of $1,000 to about thirty adults each year. You can be a full- or part-time student as long as you are pursuing a degree at an accredited college or university. For information and an application, write to Orville Redenbacher's Second Start Scholarship Program, Box 4137, Blair, NE 68009.

If you're not lucky enough to win a scholarship, auditing classes at a nearby college or community college is a smart, frugal way to further your education. Auditing makes sense if you want to learn a new subject or skill but don't plan to get a degree in it.

273. Another freebie.

It's no secret that good math skills add up to good grades in school and, later on, good job opportunities. Want to help your children learn math? Two free booklets are available from the National Council of Teachers of Mathematics (Department BHG2, 1906 Association Drive, Reston, VA 22091). Ideally, those booklets will enable you to save money by not paying for math tutors or summer school. Even better, your child might win a math scholarship, become a corporate CFO, and support you in your old age!

274. Educate and entertain at the same time.

Buy reasonably priced ($2–$4) Bellerophon coloring books, which provide enjoyment while presenting lessons in history, the arts, and literature. The attractive books are filled with facts, anecdotes, and exactly the kind of historical trivia that delights as much as it informs. The wide range of subjects includes great explorers, ancient Rome, ancient Africa, legends of the Vikings, dragons, dinosaurs, Shakespeare, Amelia Earhart, and much more. Contact Bellerophon Books at 36 Anacapa Street, Santa Barbara, CA 93101 (805-965-7034) and request a catalog.

275. Browse used bookstores.

If you want to buy a few enjoyable paperbacks and don't mind what shape they're in, try used bookstores—they're great places to find little-known works by well-known authors as well as most popular fiction. Also, charitable organizations and libraries in many communities offer annual book sales where you can get most paperbacks for 50 cents, hardcovers for $1 or $2—and on the last day of the sale, an entire brown bag of books for $2 or $3! That should take care of your summer reading—and the rest of the year as well.

> AAUW (the American Association of University Women) has hundreds of U.S. chapters that sponsor book sales and other fund-raisers annually to raise money for scholarships for women. To support this good cause and find out if your community has an AAUW branch that holds used book sales, check your phone book or contact AAUW's national office at: 2401 Virginia Avenue NW, Washington, DC 20037 (202-785-7700).

276. Live in a district with a good school.

Get a smaller house if you have to, but always buy into a good school district. If you have children, your return will be immediate in terms of a superior education and the enrichment and after-school and summer programs that usually go with it—programs you would be hard put to duplicate out of private funds. Even if you don't have kids, still look in areas with reputations for good schools, because these neighborhoods tend to remain more desirable over time and retain their value even in down real estate markets.

277. Spend time, not money.

The best investment you can make in your kids' education is giving them lots of your time and attention—the more, the better. The earlier you start reading to your kids, making sure they see you read, taking them to museum exhibits, limiting TV viewing, talking with them about weighty issues, traveling to unusual destinations (both locally and nationally), and creating artworks or telling stories together, the more likely it is that your child will find learning fun and exciting. Most of these are free family activities that can lead to success in school and later in life.

278. Join a Scholastic Book Club.

If you like to buy books for your children, these clubs are a great bargain. You are never locked into extra purchases—you just have the option each month of choosing from dozens of well-regarded kids' books at prices well below publishers' list prices. You often can find paperbacks from 99 cents to $4; occasionally you can get $10 off a lovely hardcover and use it for gift-giving. Most parents or teachers of school-age kids can tell you how to get on the list for receiving the book club leaflets; there is a special Trumpet Club for preschoolers and toddlers as well.

279. Get help for college financing.

If you have college-bound kids, the best no-cost (how's that for cheap!) call you can make is to 1-800-572-5580. Request the guide that explains the numerous types of grants, loans, and scholarships available. You also can write to the U.S. Department of Education, Pueblo, CO 81009, and request any and all information relating to college finances.

280. Another freebie.

Use the library for books and magazines. Even small suburban libraries carry more than 100 magazines, and all you have to do to get a book that isn't on the shelves is to request it from interlibrary loan. Taking your kids to the library to choose new books every couple of weeks can be a delightful family time—and wonderfully economical. Martha recently checked out ten storybooks for her two children. When she added up their prices, she realized that she would have spent $127.50 if she'd bought them at a bookstore. Instead, she and the kids read these books dozens

Our adult reading list last week, all free of charge courtesy of the local library, included *The Atlantic* (which costs $18 annually), *Newsweek* ($46), *People* ($86), *Metropolitan Home* ($10), and *Kiplinger's Personal Finance* ($18). To carry those subscriptions at home would cost over $175, and that's just for one week's reading! Next time we're looking forward to reading *Smithsonian, Quilter's Newsletter,* and *MacWorld.*

of times in three weeks and then enjoyed choosing another stack during their next library visit.

281. Turn to family, friends, and neighbors for tutoring.

Now that many cash-strapped school districts are charging $20 to $120 for summer school make-up classes (not to mention the $25-per-hour fee private tutors cost), save by tapping the skills of friends and family. Many professionals are pleased to be asked to share their knowledge—and tutoring in a particular subject is usually a short-term commitment. And make sure a parent or older sibling is available several nights a week to supervise homework and help kids develop the good study skills that lead to success in school.

282. Shop where the schools do.

Where can you find inexpensive back-to-school supplies? You can shop by mail and get good deals from the enormous supply catalogs that schools use. They're also a great source for paint, paper, and other crafts supplies. The top two catalogs to request are from Ideal School Supply Company, 11000 South Lavergne Avenue, Oak Lawn, IL 60453 (1-800-323-5131) and J.L. Hammett, 1 Hammett Place, Braintree, MA 02184 (1-800-333-4600).

Living Better for Less

283. Pack a snack.

Ward off expensive junk food attacks while on the road. These attacks can, of course, happen at any time, but they're particularly common during long car trips. Our solution is to keep healthful "emergency" snack food such as crackers or dried fruit in the car and to pack a picnic lunch every time you hit the road for a few hours or more. You'll save about $4 apiece every time you brown-bag it, and you can enjoy something different from the same old fast food fare.

284. Exercise with the Queen.

Give up that expensive health club membership and join a cheaper YW/MCA. Even better, join the Aretha Franklin Home Aerobics Club: a half-hour of dancing in the living room to "Respect," "Chains," and "Pink Cadillac" three times a week. Some people we know club hop with Fleetwood Mac or the Doobies, but being traditionalists, we prefer the Queen.

Another exercise alternative is to borrow a two-year-old and a toddler (if you don't already have them at home) and let them run you ragged.

285. Coddle your colds for less.

When you or your children have a cold, use a simple drop of eucalyptus oil or menthol (available in health food stores if your pharmacy doesn't carry it) in your hot moist humidifier instead of expensive vapor rubs. This oil is the active agent in most rubs, anyway. Why pay over $5 for some packaging when the key ingredient is available for under $2?

286. Make the most of ingredients you already have on hand.

These cheap but effective home remedies alleviate the pain of an insect bite or sting: Use ice, a paste of baking soda and water, or any meat tenderizer containing the enzyme papain. If you apply it to the bite site immediately, the papain works to break down the protein-based venom. Baking soda also can soothe a sunburn or rash when added to your bath. Your savings? Well, Ac'cent at $1.83 for 2 ounces costs one-third as much as 2 ounces of Benadryl at $5.79.

287. Treat your feet nicely.

Buy good shoes that fit well and, whenever possible, avoid high heels. This will save you all the money you would otherwise have to spend on the remedies for headaches and sore backs resulting from ill-fitting shoes, plus the podiatrist fees for treating corns and calluses. This is especially true for children's growing feet, so don't swap shoes among siblings. Though it may be tempting, it's counterproductive in the long run.

288. Trouble getting to sleep at night?

Don't rely on expensive and potentially addictive sleeping pills or, even worse, tune in to the Home Shopping Network. Good old-fashioned warm milk may actually help, probably due to the beneficial effect of the amino acid L-tryptophan. Research has also shown that simple exercise during the day, such as a twenty-minute walk, also can help. Cutting down on your alcohol, caffeine, and nicotine consumption will dramatically reduce the influence of these artificial stimulants, which may be keeping you from getting the rest you need.

289. Catch side effects before they catch you.

Whenever you take medicine, check with your pharmacist, physician, or local library's *Physician's Desk Reference* (PDR for short) for side effects that may end up costing you time, health, and more money. Many common medications can cause adverse side effects. For instance, oral contraceptives and high blood pressure drugs that contain reserpine and hydralazine may cause headaches, and antihistamines, decongestants, and antidepressants can cause insomnia. Check before you have your prescription filled or buy that over-the-counter cold remedy—opened medicine isn't returnable, so the money you lose when you can't take a medication you've already bought is totally wasted.

To take the sting out of a fever blister, apply a cold wet tea bag. Baking soda is a great tooth cleanser when mixed with hydrogen peroxide and a small amount of salt.

290. Another freebie.

A variety of gadgets are now available to help you stretch your legs before running or other sports. You can buy a curvy plastic single-leg stretcher for $29.95 or a double stretcher for twice the price. As far as we can tell, none works better than the front stairs or a stack of books. We prefer the books, because they are adjustable.

291. Pack a peck of peas.

Use a bag of frozen peas for an ice pack. It conforms better to the shape of an arm or leg than more expensive ice packs. If you are going to a sports event, little league game, or even a beach outing or picnic, just throw the bag of peas into the cooler along with the juice and fresh fruit. At $1.29 a bag, they're $5 cheaper than an ice pack.

> **B**onus benefit: Many kids love frozen peas as a snack, so your frozen bag of peas can be useful even if everyone stays uninjured.

292. Get your dental work done at a discount.

If you have a medical or dental school near you, call to inquire if it offers health and dental services as part of its education programs. The students are usually at the senior level and very closely supervised. The same is true for hairdressing schools, if you're brave enough to try it—you can get a haircut at a very reasonable price that way.

293. Create your own home facial.

Here's how: Tie your hair back or wrap it in a shower cap or towel. Make a paste of oatmeal and water and apply it to your face, avoiding the tender skin directly around your eyes. Let it dry approximately one-half hour or until your skin feels as tight as Eva Gabor's looks. Gently rub off the oatmeal paste with a damp towel. Your skin will be as glowing as if you spent $50 in the salon (or $10 for some store-bought mud). If you invite a friend over to listen to music and gossip while you are tightening, you will have achieved the full salon treatment at a fraction of the cost.

Men who would like to do something nice for their skin but wouldn't be caught dead in a salon may also appreciate this inexpensive home version.

294. Keep a healthy lifestyle.

In the long run, preventive medicine is always cheaper than any medical bills you may incur for such unhealthy habit-related illnesses as emphysema from smoking (which can lead to spending $100 a month for oxygen plus $600 for a wheelchair), cirrhosis from drinking ($400,000 for a liver transplant), and heart disease from a high-fat diet ($250,000 for a triple bypass). The frugal fact is that cutting back on tobacco, alcohol, and fatty meat will save your money and your life.

295. Take a hard look at your vices.

They're doing damage to your budget as well as to your health. Cigarette smokers who go through twenty cigarettes a day will see $912 a year going up in smoke. Beer drinkers who imbibe two six-packs a week will be down $364 a year; wine drinkers who go through two $5 bottles of wine a week will also be out $520 at the end of the year. And drinkers of harder stuff, who indulge in a $12 bottle of scotch, gin, or equivalent a week, will shell out $624 a year. By giving up drinking and smoking, or at least cutting down on your consumption, you'll be surprised how much money will be left over to enjoy in other ways. (For instance, you'll have more to spend on really hard-core habits, such as coffee and chocolate!)

296. Smart buys save money.

Don't stint on safety equipment for sports. A routine visit to your doctor's office may cost only $30, but after a fall from a bike or a horse it's impossible to escape from the emergency room for under $200, especially if X rays or stitches are involved. So be firm about safety helmets, shin guards, knee pads, and the like (purchased at good-quality secondhand stores and garage sales, of course), and drill yourself and your children in the safety procedures appropriate to your sport.

297. Check your hospital bills *very* carefully.

In a study by the Bristol-Myers Squibb Company, 98 percent of hospital bills were found to contain errors, and the average overcharge was a whopping $1,254! Errors like that cry out for a close reading of all hospital bills, even if you are lucky enough to have your insurance company pick up a large part of the tab.

298. Take a nap.

One of the best things you can do to save money is get enough sleep. When we are tired and run down, we are more susceptible to all types of illness, and illness translates into expenditures for medication and lost work time. Parents of young children usually are chronically fatigued, which makes them even more susceptible to whatever bug little Billy brings home from play group or preschool. One good way to catch up is to trade sleep-late mornings with your spouse on the weekend—that way each of you gets a chance to catch up at least once a week.

299. Another freebie.

If allergies run in your family, try to breastfeed your infants for at least six months. Studies show that breastfeeding has a significant impact on reducing allergies, which not only make a young child's life miserable and restrict activities, but—at $50 a visit to the medical specialist, medications, and shots—can also be quite expensive.

> Assuming your child nurses until she's a year old, breastfeeding also will save you over $700 in formula, bottles, and liners.

300. Smart buys save money.

Schedule a dental exam and thorough teeth cleaning twice a year. It costs about $50 to $60 per visit, but this preventive maintenance can save you hundreds in dental bills a little farther down the road. Most dentists begin seeing children for regular checkups at age two or three, and can identify small problems with growing teeth before they become big ones. Also, don't forget to buy a new toothbrush every few months for everyone in the family.

> You may be more motivated to brush regularly when you consider that the current cost for one filling is $60 to $175, depending on the material used, and a single root canal costs $290 (up to $600 if it's in a four-root molar).

301. Prevent loss with floss.

Many adults don't know it, but they should start worrying about the condition of their gums if they're concerned about losing their teeth someday. Periodontal disease—infection of the gums caused by plaque buildup—is the leading cause of tooth loss for people over thirty-five. Brushing isn't enough. Only regular flossing, which removes the plaque at the gum line and dislodges bacteria, gets the job done right. So don't neglect your own mouth while you're teaching the kids how to care for their own teeth.

> The cost of oral surgery to repair damaged gums can be as much as $6,000, depending on the extent of the damage.

302. Who needs this?

Instead of buying bottled drinking water, there's a simple trick for making your own home's tap water taste better. If you live in an area that has well water with a strong-tasting mineral content, simply fill up a clean, empty milk jug and let it sit overnight. (We prefer to leave a jug of water in the refrigerator at all times.) Letting the water sit removes the strong taste as well as a little sediment, without your having to buy an expensive water filtration system. This method is especially effective in removing the "swimming pool" taste from heavily chlorinated water. Just avoid drinking the last inch or two of water if you see any sediment at the bottom of the jug.

303. Who needs this?

Don't spend $300 on a "Stairmaster"-type exercise machine when there are stairs available to you absolutely free. In your house, up to the office, between floors at the mall—stairs are everywhere! We heard of one staircase up to the boardwalk in Venice, California, that became so popular an exercise spot they had to install lane markers.

304. Baby your face.

Instead of buying those teeny little jars of makeup remover for $3 or $4 a pop, get a large economy bottle of baby oil for under $2. Baby oil works just as well, if not better, in removing eye makeup, and it's the major component of most cosmetic removers anyway. By buying baby oil, you won't have to pay for the added perfumes and stabilizers in the name-brand makeup removers, and you won't subject your sensitive skin to their mystery ingredients. The less makeup you get in the habit of buying

Bonus benefits of wearing little or no makeup: You can cry in the movies and not come out looking like a raccoon. You can snuggle without leaving sticky smears on the snugglee. And you'll never get in a traffic accident while checking your lipstick in the rearview mirror.

and wearing, in fact, the more money you'll save—not to mention the added bonus of being able to enjoy precious extra minutes of sleep every morning!

305. Who needs this?

We recently saw an ad for "the first and only emergency tooth preserving product for the home." For $11, you can buy a bottle of saline solution "and other nutrients"; when a child knocks out a permanent tooth, you can pop the lost tooth into the bottle and race to the dentist. This sounds great—until you look in any first-aid book and discover that a cup of cold milk is just as effective in keeping the tooth alive until the dentist can replant it.

306. Who needs this?

The latest fad device for taking your child's temperature is an electronic thermometer that instantly records the body's temperature when placed in one ear. This all sounds great until you take a peek at the price tag: a whopping $99. Now, no one enjoys holding down wiggling children and trying to get them to sit still long enough to get a good reading, but spending almost $100 on a faster device still seems ridiculous to us. (The nurse at our pediatrician's office also confided that she has serious doubts about this device's accuracy.)

If you'd like something a bit more convenient than the old traditional thermometer (Martha has to admit that she's never been able to read the darned things—those thin silver lines seem to vanish when she looks at them), you could pay a more reasonable $10 for a small electronic thermometer. It takes an underarm reading, beeps when up to temperature, and gives you a nice, clear digital number when done.

307. Try a new tack—tack shop, that is.

Looking for a fabulous deal on hand cream? No animal on earth is more pampered than a fine show horse, and tack shops carry a wide array of excellent moisturizers, detanglers, and conditioners for a fraction of the cost of those in department stores. In fact, shop owners estimate that between 65 and 80 percent of their horse-grooming products never even make it into the barn, but go straight to the bathroom. Two brands to look for are the Hoofmaker and Horseman's One Step, each priced under $7 for big 16-ounce jars. They smell great, really work, and represent a considerable savings over the $30 to $40 you would spend for a comparable amount and quality of fine hand lotion. We've also heard rave reviews of Mane 'n' Tail hair conditioner.

If you don't have access to tack shops, here's another idea you can try. Buy an aloe plant and put it in a sunny place on your windowsill. Whenever your skin feels dry, break off one of the plant's stems, squeeze it, and rub the natural moisturizer onto your hands, face, or legs. Aloe is a primary ingredient of many moisturizers; it also relieves itching from rashes or insect bites and soothes sunburns. By growing your own, you can benefit from the aloe without having to pay for all those mysterious additives in store-bought creams and lotions.

308. Splurge on a sponge.

Everyone knows natural sponges can't be beat for makeup removal, home painting projects such as wall texturing, or craftwork on pottery and fabrics. But with even small specimens going for $5 to $7, who can afford them? You can if you order them from State Line Tack in Plaistow, New Hampshire (1-800-228-9208). Their large sponges are under $10, with small ones priced at an unbelievable $1.99.

309. Pick your pharmacy carefully.

Most of us know that it's a smart idea to ask pharmacists for the generic version of any prescription medicine we need. (Some prescription tranquilizers, for example, can cost as much as $1.25 per pill—or you can buy the generic version for a nickel apiece!) But did you know that pharmacy drug prices vary as widely? Calling around to two or three local pharmacies before you get your prescription filled can save you $10 to $30 each time you're sick.

310. Who needs this?

If you already own a bicycle, you don't need to buy an indoor exercise bike. You can buy a bike stand with adjustable tension for around $100 at a bicycle or sporting goods store, hook up your own bike, and ride it indoors in bad weather. By contrast, some exercycles, such as Schwinn's trendy AirDyne, cost as much as $599.

This is a wonderful way for avid bikers to train during the winter months as well as a useful way for less-than-athletic types to get rid of some excess pounds. The best part is that you can unhook your bike and ride away on a nice spring day, which is more than you can do with the expensive exercycle.

311. Who needs this?

There's only one thing wrong with the major diet programs, according to *Consumer Reports*—they don't work very well. None of the popular dieting programs the magazine studied was successful in enabling dieters to keep the weight off over the long run. And the cost of these programs is astonishing. The Jenny Craig weight loss program, for example, can cost $208 per year—plus $3.50 for each one of their meals, which they strongly suggest you need to buy. (That'll add up to $2,555, if you buy two meals a day for a year.) No wonder it's a $3 billion industry! Instead of signing up for Nutri-System or Jenny Craig, try to eat smaller portions of the meals you cook at home.

312. Make your own long-lasting ashtrays.

The black bottom part of two-liter plastic soda bottles makes great ashtrays. Simply cut the bottom off the bottle with a sharp knife or pair of scissors. If you don't allow smoking in your home because you're worried about secondhand smoke or can't stand the smell, scatter these ashtrays on your deck or patio. They're completely waterproof, so can stand up to rainstorms, and you won't have to spend a cent on a habit you disapprove of.

313. Donate your blood to yourself.

Save money on surgical procedures (and reduce any contamination-related anxieties you might have) by donating blood to yourself ahead of time. To find out about directed donations, write to Gloria Jones, American College of Surgeons, 55 E. Erie Street, Chicago, IL 60611, and ask for the booklet on surgery. You also can make inquiries at the hospital where the procedure is going to be done.

Keeping Pets Without Running Up Debts

314. Get a pet.

While it does cost a certain amount to keep a pet properly (vet and food bills really do add up), we've come to the conclusion that animals are worth it because they make us happier, remind us that we're not the only species on the planet, provide entertainment for the children while simultaneously teaching them responsibility, and are good foot-warmers on cold winter nights. Recent studies even indicate that pets can cure depression, especially in older folk who may be living alone, feeling isolated and in need of a good and faithful companion. Other studies have found that adults' and children's blood pressure and heart rate tend to drop when they're with their pets. When you look at it that way, pets are a real bargain.

315. But take a pass on Lassie.

This may come as a shock to those of us who grew up on Lassie, but long-haired dogs (and cats) are a real bother. Not only do they require expensive professional grooming on a regular basis, but keeping them as house pets pretty much ensures that your carpets and upholstery will also need professional cleaning on a regular basis. When possible, avoid dogs that will shed all over your rugs, couch, clothes, and all your other belongings as well as play havoc with allergy sufferers.

Grooming prices at our local puppy parlor aren't cheap: One shampoo costs $25, and a shampoo and grooming costs $40. Painted toenails and bows for those poor poodles add even more expense. A short-haired dog you can groom yourself will easily save you $300 a year.

316. Skip the pet shops.

Don't buy pets from those pet shops that proliferate in malls and shopping centers. They could wind up costing you a lot of heartache and money, because the pups in these places are bred by "puppy mills," with little or no regard for sturdiness. Animals from these sources are often prone to congenital genetic problems (such as bad hips in German shepherds), and without viewing the parents, you really have no idea how that adorable pup will turn out. Two years down the road, when you are paying big bucks in vet fees or trying to explain to little Timmy why you have to put Bowser down, you'll regret giving in to that cute little face in the window.

317. Shop at animal shelters.

If you want a good dog, there are two sources. First is a reputable breeder where you can view the entire litter and see at least one of the parents. You may pay a little more initially, but it will be worth it because your animal will be healthier. The other source is an animal shelter, where you should pick out the friendliest mongrel you can find. Why a mongrel? Because you won't have

Shelters usually charge under $40 for a dog or cat, and this fee often includes vaccinations plus neutering—services that would cost twice as much at the vet.

to worry about instability of mind or body caused by inbreeding; crossbreds are almost always healthier than purebreds.

318. Training your pet can pay off.

At the very least, train your dog to walk on a leash, sit, and stay. That way you can avoid the astronomical vet bills (and the heartbreak) usually incurred when a misbehaving Fido runs into the street and gets hit by a car. An added bonus is that well-behaved dogs make it easier for you to get friends to sit for them when you're away, thereby avoiding exorbitant boarding fees. Teaching one incredibly cute trick—such as balancing a cheese cracker on the nose (the dog's, not yours)—also helps make your pet a more attractive house guest.

319. Always neuter your pets.

Not only will it save you the time and trouble of finding homes for all those unwanted puppies and kittens, but it also will prevent the hundreds of dollars in vet fees it will cost you to have Fido or Fluffy sewn up after a heavy date night. It's also healthier for the animals in the long run.

320. Keep your cats on a low-ash diet.

High ash content in food is a main contributor to feline urinary syndrome, a chronic bladder condition that, while common and treatable, is expensive to cure. Between tests and medication your bill can easily come to $100. While special foods cost more than the cheap dry brands, they often are available by the case from discount pet food stores and the large animal feed stores that supply kennels, farms, and catteries.

The most expensive cat food source is often your vet. Darcie's vet charges $33 for a case of Science Diet Feline Maintenance cat food that she can get from the feed supply store for $26. Since her cat goes through a case a month, we figure that Darcie saves $84 on pet food per year, plus the $200 she saves by preventing feline illness. If you have more cats, you'll save even more.

321. Use better bedding.

If your kids are keen on what Darcie calls "varmints"—hamsters, guinea pigs, and the like—you are probably paying ridiculous prices for cage bedding. Search through your local Yellow Pages for a tack and feed store of the horsey variety and buy your shavings there. You will pay $3.50 for a huge bagged bale of the stuff (about 4 cubic feet), which is cheaper than the small plastic pouch found in the pet stores. Four cubic feet should last you all year and save close to $90 in bedding costs. If the bale outlasts the lifetime of the pets, well, it makes great mulch around the roses too.

322. Clip those claws yourself.

Use this simple trick to trim your cat's claws yourself with a regular nail clipper: First wrap the cat in a towel. (Use a large heavy bath towel, not a thin little kitchen towel, or else you'll end up getting scratched anyhow.) Leave the cat's head and whatever leg you are working on out of the wrap, hold kitty on your lap with her head facing away from you, squeeze the paw very gently to splay the claws, and commence trimming. Be careful not to cut as far up as the big vein that runs through each claw—all you really need to take off is the sharp tip.

This procedure is safe, easy, and shouldn't take more than ten minutes once you get the hang of it. Assuming your groomer charges $20 for this service, you could save up to $240 a year in cat care. And that buys a lot of kitty litter.

323. Fight fleas the easy way.

If you live in a rural area and your animals run in and out of the house all day, come August you're probably engaged in some pretty heavy-duty flea fighting. All that bombing and spraying can cost a lot, not just in money but also in terms of the amount of chemicals you're spreading around your house and in your pet's system. In our experience, the single best—and cheapest—thing you can do to help control pet fleas is to vacuum. Honest. The real breeding ground for fleas isn't on your pets, but in your carpets and couch. Daily cleaning helps to keep things in control so that you can get by with fewer sprays and insecticidal bombs.

324. Who needs this?

We were amused to come across a nonslip, heavy-duty plastic dog bathtub with hose, drain, and detachable showerhead for $99.95 in a catalog recently. We favor the cheap plastic wading pool or traditional home bathtub option instead. Does your dog really need a more advanced shower/bath than you? (The same goes for pampering your pooch with soft feather beds when you're still sleeping on a lumpy twelve-year-old mattress.)

325. Craft your own hutch with a camper top.

For some reason old camper tops really bring out the creative urge in recyclers—we've seen them resurrected as planters, sandboxes, cold frames, and doll houses. *Mother Jones* magazine suggests that you transform one into a portable hutch for young chicks and ducks by building a simple plywood box to support the top. The advantage of using an old camper top instead of finishing off the hutch in wood is that, in addition to being free (or almost free if you get it from the junkyard), it already has built-in operating windows and doors to regulate temperature and control indoor/outdoor access for the little critters. Brand-new, store-bought hutches with these features can cost as much as $100.

If you're not in the bird business, consider using the hutch for pups, kittens, rabbits, or any other outdoor pet.

326. Better yet, borrow a pet.

Anyone who is concerned about the cost of keeping a pet, or who suffers from allergies to animals, might want to subscribe to the Bullen family theory of pets. That is, enjoy all the pets who live nearby. Pet-sit, on occasion, for a friend or offer to take the rabbit or guinea pig home from preschool for a long weekend. Play catch with friendly dogs that are walking through the park, and take the time to pat a neighbor's cat. You and your kids can have fun romping with other people's animals and then happily return to your quiet, odor-free home (which is also not covered with dog or cat hairs). You won't have to shell out for pet food, shots, vet bills, licenses, and the like. Martha's family has dogs living on all three sides of their house, so they feel no need to buy one of their own.

327. Do not ask for whom the worm turns.

Here's a low-maintenance, completely free pet you may not have thought of before: worms. Really, we're serious about this. Martha's daughter Claire recently took an old sand bucket, went out behind the garage, and dug and dug until she encountered ten worms. She greeted each find with squeals of delight, gave each a name (Patch, Squiggly, Squirmy, Dirty, Bubbly, Spot, Mucky, Corey, Jenny, and Elizabeth), and carefully placed each worm in fresh dirt in her bucket. Then we put plastic wrap over the top of the bucket, (don't forget to secure the plastic wrap with a rubber band), carefully poked in air holes, and were done. (Add a little fresh water and table scraps once a week to keep the worms wiggling.) She's so enamored of her new worms that she holds their bucket while watching TV (and during dinner, but we put a stop to that one). If your child has been pleading for a pet, helping him or her dig for a worm family may get you off the hook.

328. Get double duty for your dollars.

If you have cats and enjoy growing flowers, you can make kitty litter go farther by using it to dry flowers. Take a used coffee can or cookie tin and fill it with alternate layers of flowers and any brand of clumping-type kitty litter. Cover it tightly and leave it undisturbed. One week later, open up the can. You'll find beautifully preserved flowers with remarkably bright colors, plus your next week's supply of cat box filler.

Affordable Fun for Every Day and Holidays

329. Don't be a "vidiot" when it comes to tapes.

Our local video store rents tapes for only $1 and $2. We asked the owner how he could possibly make a profit with such a low rental fee. He explained that it isn't the one-night rentals he makes his money on, but the incredible late fee charges that build up when people forget to return the tapes on time. He has had teenagers bring back a batch of four or five tapes up to a week late for some truly exorbitant fees. So, make a point to remember to bring back those videos by developing some sort of reminder—perhaps a "RETURN TAPES" note on the door.

> We simply take the plastic cases the videos come in and leave them on the floor by the front door when we remove the tape to play it. Stubbed toes are a great instant reminder.

330. Another freebie.

Remember to take time to enjoy the simple pleasures of life—from taking a stroll with a child to sharing a cup of coffee with a friend. Savoring these moments can make for lasting happy memories, unlike those days spent frantically searching for activities and excitement at the mall or an amusement park.

331. Save money on vacation souvenirs by making your own.

It only takes a few vacation trips with the kids for parents to realize that they could probably spend a week in Hawaii with all the money spent on tacky souvenirs. Before a trip, purchase a variety of wide, cheap, undecorated plastic bracelets and barrettes and blank notebooks or scrap books from a drugstore, as well as small plain boxes you can get for free from your box stash. You also will need white glue and tweezers. On your trip, collect shells, leaves, pebbles, and postcards to decorate these items. You will have a great memento from your trip—plus it's personalized. You'll spend less than $10 by buying the materials, and you can make a wide assortment of souvenirs. By contrast, ten bucks would barely buy one item from a vacation gift shop.

Your school-age kids can have the fun of creating their own vacation or summer scrapbook if you give them a cheap little plastic camera before your trip. They'll have the chance to learn how to compose a photograph and can record their favorite experiences at the same time.

332. Wing it.

Birdwatching can provide hours of viewing pleasure for the whole family. If you garden, the easiest way to attract birds is to plant the plants that are attractive to them, then sit back and enjoy the free show. (You can enjoy the plants too, of course!) Since each seed packet costs between 99 cents and $2, the start-up costs for your garden are very low.

If you don't have a garden, a stake or window-mount feeder will be just as welcoming to your feathered friends. With the

The birdwatcher's garden should include any of the following; Shrubs: dogwood, holly, honeysuckle, pyracantha, viburnum; Annuals: cosmos; salvia, sunflowers, and zinnia; Perennials: foxglove and monarda.

addition of a few field guides from the library, you'll be able to start an activity that will give your children pleasure for their entire lives.

333. Purchase some puzzles.

Few games can provide more hours of cheap family or individual fun than a good puzzle. Compared to video games, puzzles are thrifty ($15 vs. $69), can be played by an unlimited number of people, don't cost electricity to operate, and are quiet, quiet, quiet. If you've already exhausted the usual supply of Taj Mahal and New England bridge designs available in your local toy store or supermarket, consider ordering something more unique and challenging from the Bits & Pieces puzzle catalog. Besides exotic places, its selection includes puzzles of Fabergé eggs, African wildlife, and M. C. Escher's visual jokes. Contact the company at 1 Puzzle Place, Stevens Point, WI 54481 (1-800-544-7297).

334. Who needs this?

Don't go overboard on kids' birthday parties with clowns, magicians, and elaborate party favors. Your basic clown or magician charges between $80 and $100 to entertain a small group of kids; having a birthday party at an indoor amusement center like the Discovery Zone costs a minimum of $10 per child. Even worse, with these kinds of elaborate birthday parties, the birthday child is often overwhelmed with all the excitment and ends up in tears. And you end up kicking yourself for all the money you spent.

We've learned that for preschool children, the ideal party is one in which they are allowed to roll around in mud, paint on the walls, eat pudding with their hands, or frost their own cupcakes. (If you just warn the other parents ahead of time that the children will be hosed off before returning, they might not start referring to your home as "that pigsty down the street.")

For slightly older children, nothing beats taking a picnic out to the local playground and having a few organized games, such as Blind Man's Buff and Pin the Tail on the Donkey (or Pin the Nose on Mickey Mouse). Indoor birthday parties can revolve around a communal puppet show, treasure hunt, balloon volleyball, or dress-up party. Most of these parties can be held for no more than $10 or $15, which includes the cost of your homemade cake. And remember—if you spoil your preschooler and raise the stakes each time she has a birthday, she may expect an entire brass band and her own three-ring circus when she reaches the ripe old age of twelve.

335. Use it twice for half the price.

Keep old belts, scarves, jewelry, lingerie, makeup, and so on for rainy days and costume parties. If you have children, this sort of dress-up box is the ideal birthday or holiday gift—and all the components can be bought from resale shops, of course! Darcie's grandparents often used such a box to keep the grandchildren entertained while the adults gossiped and played cards in the next room. Every few minutes a new costume would be paraded

Who needs this? You can buy a dress-up box with ten outfits in a cardboard "trunk" from Lillian Vernon for $39.98, from the Reader's Digest Kids catalog for a mere $54.98—or you can get one for the truly eye-popping price of $125 from Bloomingale's! On the other hand, you can make your own for under $10 by smart shopping at resale shops and garage sales, and by raiding your own closet. Store these dress-up clothes in an old suitcase.

and applauded, and then the kids would go back to the box while the adults returned to their cards. Everyone seemed happy with this arrangement.

336. Another freebie.

We recently sent away for some brochures on wooden backyard "play systems" and were astonished to discover that prices for a fairly basic model started at $1,700 (plus $350 for delivery and installation). The more elaborate models cost as much as $5,000! This seems a ridiculous price to pay for something your kids will outgrow in a few short years. If you have a small or nonexistent yard, or if you want to avoid spending this kind of money on a swing set, try going to different community parks instead. You'll all enjoy the variety, and they're absolutely free.

337. Save on sand play.

This same advice applies about buying a sandbox. You can save up to $100 by heading to your local playground instead of buying a large wooden sandbox. Most community parks have a sand area where children can get grubby and grainy to their hearts' content. They're also less likely to track gallons of sand into your living room!

Here's a creative alternative for indoor sand play that is less messy than regular sand. Fill a large plastic container, a large roasting pan, or old plastic wading pool with dried rice, small pasta shapes, birdseed, or dried beans and throw in plenty of buckets and scoops. Store these in a corner of your kitchen, playroom, or basement. If you keep a plastic sheet or old newspaper under this play area, clean-up won't be too much of a problem. This is a great way to keep kids happy in dreary weather.

338. Another freebie.

Memorize all the "Free Admission Days" at your metropolitan area's zoos, museums, kids' museums, amusement parks, and so on (or put the list up on your family bulletin board), and plan your outings accordingly.

> It's hard to take advantage of this tip if you're an employed parent—the majority of museum free days are on Tuesdays and Thursdays. You could still enjoy these special free outings on occasion by being selective about when you take your vacation days. For instance, in our town if two parents and two kids go to the art museum on Saturday, it's $24 just to get in the door; for the nearby aquarium, the entry fee is a whopping $32 per family. Take half a vacation day and go on a Tuesday afternoon, and it's all free.

339. Avoid store-bought greeting cards.

At nearly $2.75 a pop, they can cost a significant chunk of change if you buy cards every time a friend moves or has a birthday, a new job, a new baby, and so on. Instead, you can buy packs of blank cards (you can get attractive cards through UNICEF that cost just 50 cents apiece) and personalize them yourself Miss Manners says that generic, preprinted cards are against the

> Little scribblers really can save big bucks. At $1.50 a card and $3 a roll of paper, the average ten-person birthday party costs you more than $20 just for paper goods. Martha's nieces made fabulous cards by photocopying pictures of themselves and then folding over the 8½ by 11 sheet to create a self-mailer. For 10 cents a copy, they created a card that was both personal and thrifty.

rules of etiquette, anyway. Or create your own cards—ask your kids to draw their own greeting cards and wrapping paper for friends' and families' birthday parties. Their creativity will be much admired, and you'll save a bundle.

340. Another freebie.

Your local library probably carries much more than books. Many libraries let you to check out children's puzzles, audiotapes, puppets, and videotapes—perfect for a rainy day (or a long summer vacation). A recent trip provided us with a Thomas the Tank Engine puzzle ($9), two song tapes ($24), and one Sesame Street video ($15). Even assuming we take out children's entertainment just once a month, our library saves us at least $500 a year.

341. A double freebie.

Pick up a copy of a free parenting newspaper (such as *The Boston Parents' Paper* or *Chicago Parent*) if there's one published in your metropolitan area. These newspapers usually list dozens of free activities and places to go with kids each month as well as helpful articles on child rearing. Often the newspapers can be found in libraries, toy stores, kids' clothing stores, and other retail outlets where families shop. These publications are especially valuable to families who don't have an extra dime to spend on entertainment.

342. Find free story times.

Libraries often have free story hours for young kids. Many independent booksellers and large bookstore chains (such as Barnes & Noble) also offer a weekly story time.

343. Teach your kids how to have fun without spending money.

Have an alternative to going to the mall or playing Nintendo—plan a "family night" once a week at home. Depending on your children's ages, you can play tag or card games; teach the kids

Monopoly, Scrabble, checkers, or chess; catch fireflies; sing songs; watch a family movie; or just sit down and talk to each other. Children thrive on this kind of sustained attention.

344. Use it twice for half the price.

After dyeing Easter eggs, save the dye in plastic containers with tight-fitting lids. It can be used to make great watercolor paintings—if you don't mind them smelling strongly of vinegar, that is.

345. Sleep cheap.

If you're on vacation and are looking for a reasonable place to stay that is still clean and comfortable, read on. According to *Money* magazine, the best of the bunch are the Comfort Inn, Super 8, Travel Lodge, Hampton Inn, La Quinta Inn, and the Fairfield Inn. Most of these motels have pools and offer free continental breakfasts, some have restaurants, and all charge between $30 and $90. Compared to the $100 and up most hotels charge, plus the outrageous prices of hotel food ($10 for scrambled eggs, bacon, and coffee is not unusual), a discount room with a free continental breakfast is a real bargain.

> **D**iscount programs aren't always advertised—make it a habit routinely to ask for any special weekend, senior, or club rates that may apply when you make a reservation or check-in.

346. Use it twice for half the price.

Show your kids how to string their own popcorn and cranberry Christmas tree garlands with a needle and long piece of thread (but don't try this if you have any toddlers in the house who might choke on them). Then leave the strings on a tree outside for the birds to enjoy after the holidays.

Here's a use for all those holiday cards you receive every year. Give your kids some safety scissors and encourage them to cut out their favorite pictures from the cards. Once they do that, they can use a glue stick and colored paper and make a homemade book or some cards of their own. These cards work beautifully for thank-you notes. You also can have your kids make their own gift tags for next year's gift-giving by gluing some of their smaller cut-out pictures onto small pieces of cardboard.

347. Use it twice for half the price.

Save items that are not easily recycled (including laundry boxes, yarn and ribbon, a variety of colorful buttons, plastic bottle tops, foil, etc.) and give them to your kids, along with a glue stick, to make junk collages or sculptures. These materials also can be used to make colorful paper bag puppets, which are a terrific indoor activity on bad-weather days. Or make sock puppets with those mismatched pairs of socks you've been wondering what to do with.

348. You don't have to fly to earn frequent flyer miles.

Many airlines have tie-in or buy-in programs that can bring you just the extra miles you need to qualify for a free trip. For example, Northwest and American let you earn miles when you make calls on the long-distance carrier MCI, and TWA credits you with bonus miles when you send packages via its air freight service You also can earn miles by carefully choosing the hotel, rental car company, or credit card that participates in your favorite airline's plan. These special arrangements change constantly, so it's a good idea to check in with the frequent flier desk of the airline in question to see what the current programs are.

Here's a couple of examples of the leading airlines' mileage partners. American Airlines' partners include Sheraton, Hilton, Marriott, and InterContinental hotels; Avis Rent-a-Car and Hertz; Canadian Airlines; and Citibank credit cards. Call American at 1-800-882-8880 for more information on joining its program. United Airlines is in partnership with Alamo Rent-a-Car, Dollar Rent-a-Car, Hertz, and National Car Rental; Hilton, Hyatt, Westin, and Sheraton hotels; Air Canada, KLM, Air France, and Lufthansa. Contact United at 1-800-241-6522.

If you don't stay in pricey hotels often, you'll be pleased to hear that Holiday Inn recently announced that it is offering mileage awards with United, Delta, and Northwest Airlines. By paying a small fee to join the program, guests will receive 2.5 miles for each dollar spent on room rates.

349. Give yourself an allowance.

To prevent overspending on hobbies, couples can give each other an equal allowance at the beginning of each month to be spent as they each desire. In one family we know, the husband spends his allowance on computer books and woodworking tools, and the wife uses most of her spending money to buy books. They've found this a good solution—neither resents the other's "frivolous" purchases as long as they stay within their budgeted amount each month.

350. Give your kids the gift of your presence.

When your children's birthdays roll around, consider giving them a gift of special time with you instead of a costly present (which may just end up attracting dust in their bedroom). Small kids will love a trip to the zoo or a fun fair together; older children might enjoy a fishing or camping trip or a visit to a brand-new movie and ice cream parlor. For example, an afternoon at the local movie theater and a double-scoop ice cream cone for two will cost less than $10—compared to $50 for a flimsy plastic Barbie house that falls apart when you breathe on it or a Nintendo game that teaches your children 300 ways to maim and kill.

Make your child an elaborate handmade certificate promising a special day out together (which should come as close to the birthday as possible), and remember to bring along a camera to document the event. That way the child will have the outing, the memory, and a keepsake. Don't be afraid of repetition—that's how family traditions are made. Darcie's grandfather always took her to visit the fire station on her birthday. She remembers these trips with greater fondness than any toy firetruck she ever had.

351. Go to matinee shows and second-run theaters.

In our neighborhood you often can find a show for $1 or $1.50. That's even cheaper than renting a video.

Movie treats are outrageously expensive—at our local popcorn palace, a medium carton of popcorn costs $3—$1 more than the admission! Why not pop your own at home and bring it in a paper bag to munch during the movie? We greatly admire a friend who has a large collection of big fashionable African bags that she regularly uses to sneak her own movie munchies into the theater. (The night she pulled out a corned beef sandwich, we did, however, feel she was carrying things a little too far.)

352. Make a movie.

Use your videocamera to make a movie instead of going to one. For the cost of a $3 tape, you'll get hours of viewing pleasure and entertainment again and again. (Of course, home movies get incredibly tedious after a while, if all your family does is stand there woodenly and wave at the camera. Instead, you can steal a story line from a favorite play, song, or fairy tale and act it out—making full use of your dress-up box for costumes, naturally.)

353. Use it twice for half the price.

Reuse your old junk mail for scrap paper. Many coupon mailings are printed on only one side, which makes the other side perfect for scribbling on. You can keep this kind of junk mail by your phones, or use it for collages, art projects, or packing material when sending packages. In fact, most of this book was written on little scraps of paper scattered all over our houses, bathrooms, and cars. This kind of paper is also great for leaving little messages or love notes to your spouse or kids—though we draw the line at using it for stationery, as one of our friends does.

354. Another freebie.

We know a woman whose family income went from $70k a year to $30k when she quit her job to stay home with the kids. "Now I'm scared to go out of the house," she said, "because every time I go out it seems like I spend money we don't have." If you're in the same boat, don't despair—there are lots of fun places to go that don't require spending money. Some of our favorite free things to do outside the house include taking our kids on a neighborhood scavenger hunt (find a maple leaf, a blue car, a red car, a person wearing a hat, etc.); searching for the best sledding hills in wintertime and the best community parks and playgrounds in fine weather; visiting our community fire station, a nearby farm, or airport; and feeding bread crusts to the ducks at a local lake or river.

355. The best summertime fun is (nearly) free.

If you have young children, fill up a cheap plastic wading pool, get out a bottle of your homemade bubbles, a rubber ball, some colored chalk, and a shovel for digging in the dirt—and invite a few neighbors' kids over. For an extra treat, serve some homemade ice pops. Add watermelon slices for a seed-spitting contest, and you have the makings of a perfect summer day. Since going to a community swimming pool or waterpark can cost $5 to $10 apiece—and buying ice pops and snacks while you're there will cost a similar amount—we prefer this kind of backyard fun.

356. When it comes to Christmas, simplify, simplify, simplify.

Give yourself a gift by jettisoning a few of the more time-consuming, expensive holiday celebrations each year. The less frenzied you feel—and the less impoverished—the more you can enjoy the season. Here are several ways you can start:

- Don't buy the biggest Christmas tree on the lot. A tabletop artificial tree can be perfect if you often spend the holidays visiting at relatives' houses or if you have toddlers at home who would jump at the opportunity for some indoor tree climbing. (Psst—smaller trees also can look great with fewer decorations!)
- Don't shell out $40 for a dressy "tree skirt." (Martha's family uses an old, sap-stained white sheet to cover up the base of the tree every year. It works perfectly well and is not even visible after presents are added.)
- Don't illuminate your whole neighborhood; your house will look elegant and festive if you put an electric candle in each window facing the street, or use red and green light bulbs in your outdoor lights. This use of lights is discreet, traditional, and won't put a dent in your electric bill.
- Focus on the family activities that are most rewarding, instead of running from store to store until you drop. Go caroling or attend a "Sing-Along Messiah," read Christmas stories together, or watch a favorite movie in front of the fire.
- Give your young children many small, inexpensive presents instead of one or two extravagant ones. Small kids love the anticipation of unwrapping gifts and don't really care

what's inside their packages. For example, most children will be ecstatic if you give them half a dozen individually wrapped plastic dinosaurs or zoo animals.

• When your extended family multiplies, draw names for gift-giving instead of buying presents for the whole kit and caboodle.

• Save the stick-on ribbons from gifts: With a bit of folded-over Scotch tape on the back, they can be reused indefinitely and no one will ever know.

357. Go garage sale-ing.

One of the very best sources of kids' toys (besides grandparents) is garage sales. When Martha's driving around town, she tries to stop at a garage sale if there's a crib, trike, or plastic slide by the driveway. That's usually a strong hint that good pickings for kids are available. Martha has bought her daughter Claire's very favorite toys this way: a fuzzy giraffe puppet (50 cents), a cuddly rag doll ($1), and tons of costume jewelry and dress-ups (between 5 and 75 cents each). And once they were lucky enough to stumble on a Barbie extravaganza. A teenager had three full tables of Barbies displayed, along with endless piles of clothes and tiny shoes. Claire was thrilled when the "Wedding Barbie" she had her heart set on was there in great condition for $3. (We saved $17 that day by not buying a brand-new Barbie.) Be choosy, though—avoid the board games with missing pieces and the precolored coloring books. With this caveat, garage sales can be a happy hunting ground for frugal parents.

358. Use it twice for half the price.

Want a set of great roly-poly toys for your toddler for absolutely free? Save three or four panty hose "egg" containers and put a different noise-producing object in the bottom of each one. For example, you could put a bell in one, some dried beans in another, and pebbles in a third. Glue each egg's top back on

If you're having a party for kids and want to provide favors plus a fun activity, collect enough eggs for each child to make his or her own toy. Offer them several choices of fillings and colors, but make sure adults are around to help supervise the gluing part.

securely, let it dry, and then decorate with indelible markers. You'll save around $10 by not getting a similar store-bought toy.

359. Drum up some fun.

If you buy your coffee in cans, you have on hand the makings of a great percussion set for your kids. Clean four empty cans carefully and make sure there are no sharp edges on the rims. Make a shaking instrument out of the first by filling it one-quarter full of dried beans or pebbles and then gluing the plastic top back on the can to keep the contents from escaping. Use the second as a skin drum by standing it right side up with the plastic lid on—the lid is the hitting surface. Turn the third into a steel drum by turning it upside down so that the metal bottom is the hitting surface. The last can can quickly become a hanging gong if you punch a hole through the bottom, tie a knot at the end of a string, and then thread the string through the hole.

These drums can all be "tuned" to different sounds by putting a variety of objects in the canisters. Besides beans, you can experiment with sand, crumpled paper, and cloth.

360. Never lose a crayon again.

We all love to see our kids happily scribbling away at their drawing pads, but you could probably afford to buy a Picasso with the money spent replacing "lost" crayons (not to mention the pain and suffering moms endure tripping over scattered crayons or crawling under furniture looking for lost pencils). Here's a simple and cheap trick for keeping track of drawing materials: Cut a small notch in the pencil or crayon with a knife, and tie a piece of yarn or smooth string around it. (The notch is important because it keeps the string from slipping off.) Tape the other end of the string to the easel or tie it around the spiral of the drawing pad. No more lost pencils or crayons!

A bonus benefit of this trick is that you also have no more murals on the walls! This method also works perfectly when you're traveling, since retrieving crayons that have fallen under cramped airplane or car seats is just about impossible.

361. Have a cave-in in your kitchen.

Parents of crawlers and toddlers soon learn that they have to lock the bottom cabinets in their kitchens or move dangerous lotions, potions, and foodstuffs to higher storage areas. But what to do with the empty bottom cabinets? Why not revamp them as play spaces? Take the doors off the hinges, place a soft old quilt or a few towels in the bottom, and you've got a great cave play space where children can amuse themselves. They'll be out from underfoot but safely in sight while the adults prepare dinner.

We have seen all sorts of attractive children's toy boxes, play mats, and cubbies advertised for as much as $100, but the reality of the situation is that inevitably the children—and the toys—will gravitate to where the action is: the kitchen. So make the most of the materials and space you already have on hand. Your children and your wallet will be happy.

After their daughter Claire dumped the kitchen linen drawer for the two hundredth time, Martin and Martha finally realized that it was *her* drawer, after all, and replaced the linens with children's books.

362. Learn to program your VCR.

Make your own videotapes of favorite shows. Why spend $12 to $20 to buy one *Barney* or *Thomas the Tank Engine* video when you can tape the shows yourself? In fact, you could fit six half-hour shows on one $1.99 blank videotape. The same holds true for adult shows—it doesn't make any sense to buy episodes of *Star Trek* or *Cheers* when you can make your own video library next time the show is rerun.

363. Don't plan disposable birthday parties.

If you buy eight small decorated paper plates from Hallmark, eight large paper plates, a paper tablecloth, and sixteen matching napkins, you'll have spent $10 on paper goods that will last for two hours, then will all have to be thrown away. Buy a stack of brightly colored plastic plates instead at your local grocery or party store. You'll pay around $1.75 for fifteen large plates and 89 cents for eighteen small plates, and you can wash and reuse them for dozens of parties to come. The same applies to buying a box of plastic forks, knives, and spoons. Don't just toss them when you're through. They'll stand up to repeated dishwasher washings and are very handy to keep at home for visitors' and young children's use.

Forget the crepe paper as well. It costs 99 cents per roll and is meant to be tossed after the party. Instead you and your child can make an old-fashioned paper chain out of colored construction paper (which sells for around $1 per pad). Just cut the paper into strips, then glue the two ends of the first strip together to make a circle. Insert the next strip through the first paper "link" in the chain and glue its ends. You can make several feet of chain in minutes, and it makes a charming party display when draped across the ceiling and adorned with balloons. When the party's over, take down the paper chain and keep it until next time—it lasts indefinitely.

364. Another freebie.

Enjoy going to the theater for free—if you become an usher Many community and metropolitan theaters have a need for volunteer ushers, who then have the opportunity to see a variety of plays and performers at no charge. Check with your local theaters to see if they need part-time or occasional volunteers.

365. A truly creative use for dryer lint.

Dryer lint makes a wonderful craft paste for super-strong papier-mâché projects. Make the paste by mixing 3 cups lint and 2 cups water in a large saucepan. Stir to mix evenly, then add ⅔ cup flour. Stir until all lumps are gone. Add 3 drops oil of wintergreen and then cook over low heat, stirring constantly, until the mixture holds together on its own and forms little peaks as you stir (exactly like Cream of Wheat). Remove the mixture from the heat, let it cool until it is comfortable to work with, and use it to create sculptures, costume jewelry, masks, or hats just as you would regular papier-mâché. Let your project dry for five days and you will have an extremely hard and durable surface, suitable for painting or further decoration.

AFTERWORD

We hope you've enjoyed reading this book as much as we enjoyed writing it. If you have discovered some creative ways of your own to save money without knocking yourself out, please share them with us, care of Crown Publishers, 201 East 50th Street, New York, New York 10022.